Building the Continental Empire

BUILDING THE CONTINENTAL EMPIRE

American Expansion from the
Revolution to the Civil War

William Earl Weeks

The American Ways Series

IVAN R. DEE   *Chicago*

Maps by Victor Thompson

Library of Congress Cataloging-in-Publication Data:
Weeks, William Earl, 1957–
    Building the continental empire : American expansion from the
    Revolution to the Civil War / William Earl Weeks : [maps by
    Victor Thompson].
        p.   cm. — (American ways series)
    Includes bibliographical references and index.
    ISBN 1-56663-135-1 (cloth). — ISBN 1-56663-136-X (paper)
      1. United States—Territorial expansion.   2. United States—
    Foreign relations—1783–1865.   I. Title.   II Series.
E179.5.W44   1996
327.73—dc20   96-24327

To my Mother

Contents

Preface

THIS BOOK IS A concise history of the creation of an American empire, of the fundamental importance of that empire to the existence of the American nation, and of how a dispute over the future of the empire led the nation to civil war. The narrative traces the new republic's expansive surge from the Revolution to the Civil War. The major focus is the period 1815–1861, the age of Manifest Destiny. This was a time of robust expansionism, when the United States built a territorial and commercial empire with unprecedented speed and ease. Yet this expansionism brought to the surface an irreconcilable difference over the institution of slavery that eventually split the Union.

My interpretation suggests that empire was, along with enhanced security, the chief motive for the creation of a union of states. An expansionist consensus unified the nation and provided the ultimate rationale for its existence. In spite of numerous disagreements, this consensus was maintained from the time of independence until the 1850s, when opposition to the acquisition of more potential slave states stymied the South's program of Latin American expansionism. The breakdown of the expansionist consensus in the 1850s was nearly synonymous with the breakdown of the nationalist consensus, and the result was civil war.

This time in America's past is both well known and mostly forgotten. Although some historians have characterized the period as a time of relative quiet in foreign affairs, the age of Manifest Destiny was in fact the most dynamic and aggressive time in the history of the American empire. In less than half a century, the people of the United States built a transcontinental territorial empire, achieved supremacy in the Western Hemisphere, and laid the foundations for twentieth-century superpower status.

This account also examines the concept of Manifest Destiny, a complex of ideas and emotions which provided an elaborate justification for both the nation and the empire. I have quoted at length from the public and private expressions of the time in order to illustrate the pungent rhetoric of Manifest Destiny and its central assumption—that the American nation and empire was divinely ordained. But the outcome was not inevitable. The tendency of some histories to treat the creation of a transcontinental empire and the establishment of U.S. hemispheric supremacy as an inescapable prelude to hegemony in the twentieth century is itself a measure of the extent to which historians have internalized the myths of Manifest Destiny.

A note on definitions: "American nation" refers to areas encompassed by the political union of states. "Imperial domain" refers to territorial possessions of the United States not yet organized into states. "American empire" refers to anywhere the idea of America is ascendant—an area the nation's founders hoped eventually would encompass the world.

The unprecedented wealth and power attained by the United States during its relatively short history challenges the imagination and has long made that history difficult to place in perspective. American nationalism and American imperialism are unique in world history and cannot be understood by comparison to other nationalisms or imperialisms. At the end of what has been termed the "American Century," the existence of an American empire is only now gaining wide acceptance.

Building the Continental Empire

1

The American Nation and Empire to 1815

"... Westward the course of empire takes its way."
—Bishop George Berkeley, 1752

THE UNITED STATES began as a vision of collective security, expansion, and prosperity. Benjamin Franklin had been among the first to perceive America's enormous possibilities in his 1751 pamphlet "Observations concerning the Increase of Mankind . . ." Franklin envisioned a time in the not too distant future when "the greatest number of Englishmen will be on this Side of the Water" and the center of the British Empire would be in North America. The continent's cornucopia of resources would allow for open-ended population growth that would create a huge market for British manufactures—that is, if the colonies could continue to expand into new territories so as to prevent the creation of a landless class.

Franklin, a dreamer and inventor as well as a land speculator, keenly understood how the huge, sparsely populated domain west of the thirteen colonies represented a unique opportunity in world history for an experiment in living.

This project sparked Franklin's imagination like no other in his long and illustrious life. He devoted his energy to the creation of a political union capable of realizing that possibility. Franklin was not alone in his speculations. Amid the crises and contentions of the eighteenth-century European colonial system, a growing number of often well-placed and well-off British colonials began to perceive the enormous potential advantages of a union of the thirteen Atlantic colonies. Unity offered three distinct benefits: the security provided by a large and growing population over an extensive and abundant territory; the material prosperity made possible by an extensive internal market; and the capacity for territorial and commercial expansion that the first two benefits implied.

By the 1750s the British North American colonists had grown accustomed to their role as a vital link in the emerging global economy. They resided in the most valuable colonies of the most powerful empire of the eighteenth century. Prosperity and relative political and economic autonomy had encouraged a feisty sense of local pride among many colonists, even as they retained a strong sense of their Britishness. The vast resources of the North American continent and its offshore waters provided abundant economic opportunity where average hardworking persons had more chances to improve their lot than anywhere else in the world.

Colonial trade restrictions, loosely enforced until the 1760s, chafed but did not outrage. Subordination to a distant government in London seemed a small price to pay for the security, prosperity, and potential growth offered by being part of the British Empire. And, in any event, few roads existed to bridge the vast cultural, economic, political, and physical distances between the individual colonies. In a day when it was far easier to sail from Boston to London by ship than to travel from

Boston to Charleston by carriage, colonial unity seemed an impossibility and loyalty to the crown inescapable for reasons of both sentiment and interest.

This happy consensus was undermined by the unsuccessful efforts of a number of colonies to expand into the region west of the Appalachian Mountains. The most conspicuous failure was that of the Ohio Company of Virginia, whose drive to expand westward into the Ohio and Mississippi river valleys foundered in the face of French and Indian resistance in 1754.

The reluctance of the British government to support these efforts militarily, and the inability of the colonists to unite their forces against a common foe, seemed to ensure that the individual colonies would be cut off from further westward expansion.

How would the western frontier continue to function as a "safety valve" to defuse economic tensions along the Atlantic coast? Declining economic opportunities and increasing social conflict needed an outlet if political upheaval was to be avoided. French control of the Mississippi and Ohio river valleys blocked that expansion—the dreaded "encirclement" feared by so many colonists. Membership in the British Empire no longer seemed a guarantee against this predicament.

Realizing this perilous situation, Franklin promoted a confederation of the British North American colonies based on the principle of "enlightened self-interest." He hoped to persuade the leaders of the individual colonies to subordinate their particular needs and interests to the common goal of security and expansion along the western frontier. Franklin did not yet advocate independence from Great Britain, but he did push for a semiautonomous colonial union within the empire that could simultaneously defend itself from attack and expand westward.

Franklin's idea for his British North American colonial

confederation apparently was inspired by his observations of the highly effective Iroquois confederacy, a loose union of Indian tribes along the Great Lakes which by collective action had established itself as a force to be reckoned with. The success of the Iroquois confederacy seemed anomalous to Franklin's sometimes ethnocentric reasoning: "It would be a very strange Thing, if *six nations* of ignorant savages should be capable of forming a scheme for such an Union . . . and yet a like Union should be impracticable for ten or a dozen *English* colonies, to whom it is more necessary, and must be more advantageous."

In July 1754 Franklin presented his idea of colonial union to a congress of representatives of the northern colonies held at Albany, New York. There he argued for the creation of a grand council empowered to levy taxes, prepare for mutual defense, facilitate westward expansion, and oversee relations with the Indians. Setting the tone for his efforts, a famous woodcut in Franklin's *Pennsylvania Gazette* suggested "Join or Die."

The representatives at Albany acknowledged the shrewdness of Franklin's plan, unanimously resolving that "a union of the colonies is absolutely necessary for their preservation." Yet the individual colonial governments zealously resisted the establishment of the strong central authority needed to implement such an ambitious program and refused to concede any part of their autonomy, despite the attractive benefits of union.

By 1756 the conflict on the western frontier between the expansionist ambitions of the North American colonists and the Indian tribes of the Ohio River valley and their French colonial allies had helped touched off a general war between France and Britain that spread to the far corners of the globe. Variously known as the Seven Years War, the French and Indian War, or, most aptly, the Great War for the Empire, it climaxed a hundred years of intermittent warfare between the two European states. Great Britain's victory resulted in the virtual expulsion of French colonialism from the Western Hemisphere, most notably Canada. The French government had also been forced in 1762 to transfer the vast Louisiana territory to Spain in order to prevent its loss to Britain. The British Empire emerged in 1763 at the height of its power; the North American colonies represented the crown jewels of that empire.

Ironically, the overwhelming triumph of 1763 created the circumstances that led to a rift between the colonies and Great Britain, eventually resulting in independence. To many colonists, the withdrawal of the French seemed to herald the possible realization of the persistent dream of westward expansion. These hopes, however, were soon dashed by the intense resistance of an alliance of Indian tribes led by Chief Pontiac and the Shawnee prophet. Attacks ravaged settlements across the frontier and forced the British to mark the trans-Appalachian region as off limits to further expansion. The so-called Proclamation Line of 1763 frankly acknowledged the inability of the colonists to defend their settlements west of the mountains and the unwillingness of the British government to help them. The colonists objected, with some logic, that their own government had accomplished what the Indians and French had not—stopping the westward movement of the Anglo-Americans.

In addition to this presumed injustice, in the years after the end of the war the British in a variety of ways reasserted a previously lax governmental authority over the colonies. The most controversial of these ways concerned schemes by Parliament to levy taxes on the colonies to help pay part of the immense war debt that threatened Britain's financial security. In theory, this did not seem unreasonable, but the arbitrary and undemocratic manner in which these taxes were levied—"taxation without representation"—impressed many colonists as but the most notorious examples of growing British tyranny. A crackdown on the colonists' illegal commerce with foreign states, in defiance of British trade restrictions, also spawned great resentment. In short, as the potential for economic expansion westward was being foreclosed, the possibilities for commerce with non-British markets were being eliminated and the cost of doing business within the empire was rising as a result of increased taxes. British policy seemed an outrage, a tyranny, and, above all, a denial of self-government. A split in both interests and sentiments loomed; tensions mounted steadily during the 1760s and 1770s.

EMPIRE AND INDEPENDENCE

Events reached a flash point in 1774 when Parliament retaliated for the wanton destruction of private property known as "the Boston Tea Party." It closed the port of Boston and placed Massachusetts under martial law. Sentiment for collective action rose throughout the colonies. It was inescapably clear to inhabitants of every colony that if Massachusetts could be singled out for an arbitrary and unjust punishment, so could they.

The First Continental Congress, convoked in 1774 to form a collective response to the perceived tyranny from afar, demonstrated the extreme reluctance of the colonies to surrender any part of their sovereignty in the name of collective action. Representatives to the body rejected a plan to establish a central authority with the power to guide and direct their common interests. Instead they proclaimed the independence of each colony from Parliament's control while doing little to secure the political unity that might make that proclamation enforceable. Union remained a distant dream.

In January 1776 Thomas Paine, a sometime ne'er-do-well, recent emigrant to America, and protégé of Franklin, introduced a new dimension to the building crisis by arguing for colonial independence and unity in straightforward, everyday language. His pamphlet *Common Sense* combined the traditional arguments for union — security, prosperity, and the potential to expand — with the perceived advantages of being a neutral independent state in a European world frequently at war. Paine argued that America's predominantly agricultural commerce constituted "the necessaries of life and will always have a market while eating is the custom of Europe." He reasoned that connection to Great Britain unnecessarily involved the North American colonists in Britain's wars, and counseled that an independent America should "steer clear of European contentions" while reaping the benefits of a free international commerce.

In addition to his "commonsensical" arguments, Paine framed the contemplated secession from British control in transcendent terms. "The cause of America is the cause of all mankind," he wrote, and his words resonated in farmhouses and alehouses across the colonies, doing much to build a critical mass of sentiment for independence. Thousands thrilled to Paine's message that "Of more worth is one honest man to society, and in the sight of God, than all the crowned ruffians that ever lived." *Common Sense* is rightfully known as the most influential pamphlet in American history in its impact on a vital public question.

Exactly how commonsensical it was, however, is doubtful. Paine's arguments that a tie to Great Britain needlessly involved the colonists in Britain's wars overlooked the fact that the Great War for the Empire had been started in no small part by the expansionist ambitions of the colonists themselves. Too, Paine's blithe encouragement of armed rebellion by thirteen disunited and poorly equipped colonies against the world's mightiest military power is in retrospect the antithesis of common sense.

Nonetheless the rhetorical power of Paine's vision touched the hearts of many, becoming one of the first examples in American history of the persuasive possibilities of mass communication. *Common Sense* made a strong case for a united "us" versus a tyrannical "them," a conceptual leap that was essential for the development of American nationalism.

In July 1776 the Declaration of Independence issued by the Second Continental Congress further elaborated national identity by justifying the revolutionary movement as the inevitable result of "the course of human events," as necessary as the movement of the planets in the heavens. The document postulated that the former hierarchy between the colonies and the mother country no longer made sense. Like a young person achieving maturity, the fledgling states moved to assume the "separate and equal station among the powers of the earth to which nature and nature's god entitled them." The Declaration of Independence bound its signatories to a common cause whose failure would mean execution for treason, and in this respect at least was a powerful glue holding their movement together.

Time has transformed the Declaration of Independence into a transcendent philosophical statement that forms the cornerstone of the American national creed. But in 1776 it was meant as a "candid" communication to the European powers, especially France, as to the revolutionary state of affairs in the colonies, in the hope of securing foreign assistance. Yet that fact should not diminish its significance. "A decent respect for the opinions of mankind" obligated the revolutionaries to make a public statement of the reasons for the break with England, but in the end the main audience for the communiqué was the American people, who themselves needed to know exactly what action was being taken and why. It would not be the last time the nation would define itself and its values by the postures it assumed on the world stage.

On the parapets of Breed's (Bunker) Hill, in the bloody footprints in the snow at Valley Forge, and at the surrender of an entire British army at Yorktown to the tune of "The World Turned Upside Down," the sense of unity created by struggle against a common foe began to foster an American nationalism. A political union of states against a common foe could be agreed upon in a conference room, but to transform people from disparate backgrounds, interests, and sentiments into a unified nation required blood sacrifice in a common cause.

In the end, however, the revolutionary struggle would have been lost had it not been for the aid and assistance of monarchical France, with whom a military alliance was made in 1778. To some American revolutionaries, aligning their struggle for self-government with one of the most reactionary regimes in Europe was a veritable deal with the devil. Yet the specter of imminent defeat gave this desperate move an aura of necessity.

French motives in aligning with the rebels were entirely selfish. The French government could not resist the chance to lay low its ancient enemy by aiding the secession of its prized colonies. Covert military aid by the French king gave way by late 1778 to formal treaties of commerce and a military alliance with the fledgling union of states. By exploiting French fears of an American reconciliation with Great Britain in the wake of the smashing victory at Saratoga, American diplomats extracted the support of the French army and navy for their struggle. The price: entanglement in European affairs. A clause in the alliance committed the United States not to make a separate peace, effectively tying the U.S. war effort to that of France. By 1780 a general conflict had broken out in which France, Spain, the Netherlands, Denmark, Sweden, and Russia joined the United States in challenging the power of Great Britain.

The American revolutionaries were fighting not only for independence. Their leaders were keenly aware that their experiment in confederated self-government required a favorable world trade environment if the potential advantages of union were to be realized. Hence they instructed their diplomats to work at all times for commercial treaties with foreign states embodying the principles outlined in the Plan of 1776, a blueprint for American diplomats written chiefly by John Adams of Massachusetts. The so-called Model Treaty was based on the principle that "free ships make free goods"—i.e., that neutral vessels (such as those of the United States) could trade unmolested with warring states in all items not deemed contraband of war. Application of the principle of "free ships make free goods" promised a revolutionary transformation of international trade. The Model Treaty committed American diplomats to seek the right to trade with the enemies of a signatory power without fear of harassment, and to negotiate whenever possible a most-favored-nation clause guaranteeing that each signatory nation would extend to the other access to its markets on the most competitive terms allowed any foreign power. Underlying these principles was the idea of "freedom of the seas"—that the oceans of the world should be unfettered highways of commerce and exchange.

The commercial treaty with France reflected all these principles, as Franklin was able to panic the French into concessions they later came to regret. The pact signified that the Americans were attempting to reform the structures of international law and international trade as well as fighting a war of independence.

Having exploited French fears of an American reconciliation with Britain, American negotiators then exploited British fears of a Franco-American alliance to secure an extraordinarily favorable peace treaty. This abrupt reversal occurred after American diplomats learned of secret French efforts to persuade the British to agree to American independence but to draw the western boundary east of the Appalachian Mountains. This would, as Franklin put it, "coop up" the United States and once again block western expansion.

Faced with this unthinkable prospect, American negotiators Franklin, Adams, and John Jay of New York pushed the British to concede independence to the Americans on very favorable terms in the hope of splitting the Franco-American alliance. To accomplish this, however, the Americans decided to give up a major demand—Canada. Such was the scope of the nation's ambition, even at this early date.

With this obstacle to a settlement removed, the British were in a position to deal. The Treaty of Paris (1783) acknowledged the independence of the thirteen colonies and conceded a western boundary along the eastern bank of the Mississippi River, immediately more than doubling the size of the thirteen colonies. America had not been "cooped up" east of the mountains; the rebellious colonists had won their independence and had acquired the vast western imperial domain they so coveted. Victory in the Revolutionary War meant, in the words of the historian Richard Van Alstyne, "empire and independence."

THE CRITICAL PERIOD

Having achieved the unparalleled feat of a successful rebellion against the world's mightiest empire, the newly independent United States faced the even more difficult task of establishing an enduring political structure. The spirit of sacrifice and common cause that had made victory possible in war was lacking in peace.

The national government, structured according to guidelines known as the Articles of Confederation, was explicitly designed to minimize the power of the central government. Comprised of a one-house legislature made up of one representative from each state, the national government could not levy taxes, draft troops, or regulate the nation's trade via a uniform tariff policy. Federal revenues could be raised only by making requests to the individual states—a method that worked imperfectly during the war and broke down entirely during the postwar era. The consequence was a national government that could not pay back the substantial debts it had incurred during the war for independence, and that lacked the power to make effective foreign policy.

The most important task assigned to the new national government was the administration of the western imperial domain acquired as a result of the Treaty of Paris. Those states without expansionist ambitions, such as Maryland, demanded that all western territorial claims be the responsibility of the national government in order to prevent any one state from assuming preeminence over the others. This placed a huge responsibility on the national government. In the Land Ordinance of 1785 and the Northwest Ordinance of 1787, the Articles of Confederation Congress outlined how the region north of the Ohio and east of the Mississippi rivers would be surveyed, sold, and prepared for statehood.

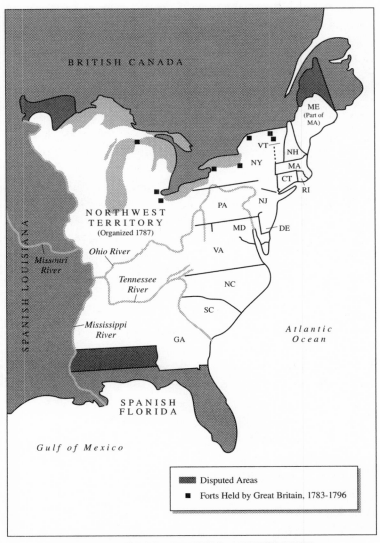

BRITISH CANADA

ME
(Part of
MA)

VT

NH

NY

MA

CT

RI

NORTHWEST
TERRITORY
(Organized 1787)

PA

NJ

Ohio River

MD

DE

VA

Missouri
River

Tennessee
River

NC

Mississippi
River

SC

SPANISH LOUISIANA

GA

Atlantic
Ocean

SPANISH
FLORIDA

Gulf of Mexico

Disputed Areas

■ Forts Held by Great Britain, 1783-1796

THE UNITED STATES AFTER THE
TREATY OF PARIS, 1783

Yet the inability of the government to manage the territory entrusted to it soon became painfully evident. Federal authority could do nothing to compel the British to evacuate a series of forts in American territory along the Great Lakes, as called for in the peace treaty of 1783. Nor could the Confederation Congress raise the troops necessary to defend settlements in the trans-Appalachian region against the attacks of the Choctaw, Shawnee, Miami, Creek, and other tribes, none of whom were reconciled to giving up their lands to the nascent American empire.

Internationally the Confederation government's inability to make a uniform national commercial policy resulted in an awkward situation. It could not retaliate against British punitive trade restrictions against American imports. Nor could it prevent individual states from engaging in import tariff wars with other states, pushing import revenues into a downward spiral.

Making matters worse, Parliament sought to punish its erstwhile subjects by closing the highly lucrative British West Indies trade to American merchants and shipping. The British West Indies market was so valuable as to prompt some Americans to question the economic advantages of independence. Lacking a center strong enough to bind the members, the union of states appeared on the verge of breaking apart.

The looming crisis of federal authority came to a head in 1786 when a tax revolt by farmers in western Massachusetts threatened the stability of the entire union. Dissident mobs led by Revolutionary War veteran Daniel Shays, angry that the state legislature aimed to pay off the state's war debt by increased taxes on cash-poor farmers, seized local courthouses and declared a moratorium on debt payments. To the consternation of much of the country's elite, no federal force existed to put down the rebellion, and state militiamen were generally sympathetic to the rebels and therefore unwilling to do much to stop Shays and his followers. Many feared the national contagion that might be precipitated by such an example. Anarchy seemed at hand.

After a good deal of hand-wringing by members of the elite, Shays's Rebellion was crushed by an impromptu military force raised by donations from wealthy individuals throughout the country. Yet in the minds of many, the crisis had crystallized the immediate peril of national dissolution under the Articles of Confederation. By early 1787 calls by the well-placed for a new national government capable of paying its debts and asserting its will both internally and externally reached a crescendo.

THE CONSTITUTIONAL COUP D'ÉTAT

A special sense of urgency drove the fifty-five men who met in Philadelphia to resolve the crises of the nation and of the empire. Empowered only to revise the Articles of Confederation, the men who met behind the boarded-up windows of what became known as Constitution Hall emerged with a complete overhaul of the terms of political union. The driving forces behind the Constitution—men such as James Madison of Virginia, Alexander Hamilton of New York, and Franklin—were determined nationalists who envisioned a powerful central authority cementing the bonds of union. In September 1787 the constitutional conspirators submitted to a series of special state ratifying conventions a plan that would fundamentally restructure national authority and, in time, transform the entire society.

The Constitution did three things that immeasurably increased federal authority. First, it gave to the federal government the power to levy direct taxes instead of relying on the "quota" system in which states were obligated but not required to donate their share of federal expenses. Now the national government could hope to maintain its financial solvency. Second, the Constitution gave the central government the power to make a uniform national commercial policy, thus ending the divisive tariff-reduction bidding wars between states for foreign commerce, and stabilizing revenues. Finally, and most significantly, it gave the new government the power to raise armies and navies, and, combined with the new taxing power, the means to support them. Overall the new Constitution erected a legal framework for an extensive political, economic, and military union with the capacity to assert its will both domestically and on the world stage.

The new Constitution also reflected a profound shift in thinking about the ideal size of a democratic republic. Heretofore the conventional wisdom held that in order to maintain their representative character, republics needed to remain small in size. A republic too large in extent would be in chronic danger of splitting apart, of a failure of the center to hold on to its far-flung parts. Now the Constitution's defenders defended their plan as a structure capable of open-ended expansion. Indeed, it was even suggested that expansion would solidify rather than weaken the Union by bringing in such a diversity of interests so as to prevent one faction, even one comprising a majority, from threatening what were considered to be, as Madison described in the Federalist Papers No. 10, the "permanent interests" of the country. Chief among these presumed "permanent interests" was the continued existence of the Union itself, which the framers of the Constitution hoped to safeguard in perpetuity.

The new plan of government made extensive provisions for the protection of private property from arbitrary seizure. A commercial society required some reasonable assurances that debts would be paid and effort rewarded. Creation of what later would be termed "a stable climate for investment" promised to facilitate internal commerce and attract foreign investors. The constitutional theorists envisioned a delicate balancing of local interests with the common needs of all the states and hoped to defend the rights of minorities (at that time, chiefly the wealthy) while embracing the principle of majority rule.

The new system did little to advance the cause of democratic rule. Indeed the Constitution was specifically structured to mute what were perceived to be the potentially irresponsible impulses of the masses at the voting booth. Franklin wrote in 1788 that "though there is a general dread of giving too much power to our governors, I think we are in more danger from too little obedience by the governed." Direct popular participation in national elections (under criteria established by the individual states) was limited to the House of Representatives. Democratic theory held that, in order to be legitimate, government required the consent of the people. This did not mean, however, that the framers of the Constitution intended that society be threatened by the presumed irresponsible whims of political majorities, such as the abolition of debts. In this regard the new regime above all promised to bring law, order, and stability to the nation.

Ratification of the Constitution occurred under conditions even less democratic than the plan itself. In a process controlled by advocates of the Constitution, a series of state ratifying conventions were called, thereby avoiding the individual state legislatures who were unlikely to vote for such a radical diminution of their power. Defenders of the Constitution styled themselves as "Federalists," thereby emphasizing a decentralized philosophy of government even as they pushed a plan whose centralizing tendencies they intentionally understated. Given the widespread popular fear of powerful central governments, it seems certain that the Constitution would never have been ratified by a direct vote of the people. In the end, backers of the Constitution pulled off a bloodless coup d'état whose arguable value cannot change the nature of its origins.

Whatever the objections to the new government, its creation soon had the intended effect of stabilizing conditions in the United States. Adoption in 1791 of Treasury Secretary Hamilton's plan for the national government to pay off at face value the debt of Congress as well as assume responsibility for the war debts of the states strengthened investor confidence in the new political entity. Many, including Madison, decried plans to repay the full value of the debt as rewarding speculators who had purchased the bonds from their original owners at a fraction of their value when the prospects of repayment appeared slim. This class of usually well-heeled and well-connected individuals who stood to profit handily from this plan became some of the new government's staunchest supporters.

In order to fund the repayment of this debt Hamilton created an extensive system of internal taxation as allowed under the new Constitution. These taxes fell disproportionately on western farmers in the form of an excise tax on distilled spirits, and kindled the outrage of many frontier farmers who relied heavily on the profits to be made from converting grain to liquor. In 1794 farmers in western Pennsylvania, in the tradition of Shays, revolted against the tax decrees of a distant and seemingly arbitrary power in what became known as the Whiskey Rebellion.

This time, unlike Shays's Rebellion, the federal government had the means to respond. The ragtag band of tax protesters melted away when confronted by the arrival in Pittsburgh of a column of fifteen thousand troops led by President George Washington. Domestic order had been decisively asserted and federal power dramatically demonstrated.

On the western frontier the newfound military prowess of the federal government was shown in August 1794 at the Battle of Fallen Timbers. A force of four thousand men under the command of General "Mad" Anthony Wayne crushed Indian resistance to American expansion in the Old Northwest. The victory paved the way for the Treaty of Fort Greenville (1795), which secured the Ohio country for the United States and ended forty years of Indian resistance in the region. Together with the Whiskey Rebellion, the victories on the western frontier signified that federal power had been made real, both in the union of states and in the western imperial domain.

THE FEDERALIST ERA

The creation of an effective apparatus of centralized power unleashed an inevitable struggle for political control of that apparatus. The framers of the Constitution had assumed that a republican government could not survive the factionalism of a multiparty state, and they drafted their document with the expectation that theirs would be the only political party. Soon, however, intense differences became apparent within the ruling Federalist party.

The course of American foreign policy proved one of the most divisive questions. Now that the federal government had the power to make an effective foreign policy, controlling its direction became of paramount importance. This division first became evident over the proper course of Anglo-American relations. The end of the war with Great Britain did not end British efforts to punish their former colonists. Trade restrictions on American commerce, continued occupation of the western forts, and complete exclusion from the highly lucrative British West Indies trade were part of a policy explicitly designed to keep the Americans in a subordinate position. As early as 1789 Madison had called, unsuccessfully, for the new Congress to retaliate by levying discriminatory import duties on British goods.

Matters escalated in February 1793 when the Anglo-French War resumed, this time as a result of the French Revolution. In an effort to cut off the French from resupply, by January 1794 the British navy seized several hundred American vessels and their cargoes. An increasingly loud and growing faction in the Congress led by Madison again called for tariff retaliation against British imports. Some even counseled a declaration of war if the ship seizures continued.

Such talk panicked those who by interest, sentiment, or some combination of the two desired to maintain close ties with Britain, whatever the outrages inflicted on the high seas. In spite of British trade restrictions, trade with Great Britain still comprised the major share of total American imports; Britain was also the most common destination for American exports. Many, including Hamilton, Washington, and most of the New England mercantile community, feared any policy that might disturb this burgeoning trade relation, destroy the basis of American prosperity, and threaten independence itself.

In order to head off the House of Representatives' efforts to retaliate commercially against Great Britain, Washington, at Hamilton's urging, dispatched John Jay to London to resolve the differences with England. Jay's Treaty (1794) gained the withdrawal of the British from the western forts, thereby depriving their Indian allies of the supplies and encouragement they needed to continue to resist the American advance. This paved the way for Wayne's victory over the Indians at Fallen Timbers and the subsequent Treaty of Fort Greenville that once and for all acquired the Ohio country for the United States. But Jay's Treaty did nothing to resolve the ship-seizure issue, nor did it assert any of America's commercial principles. Many saw it as a craven capitulation to British power, a shameful submission that disgraced the national honor. "Damn John Jay!" arose a popular cry. "Damn every one that won't damn John Jay!! Damn every one that won't put lights in his window and sit up all night damning John Jay!" Even the esteemed Washington came in for attack, and ratification of the treaty by the Senate seemed in doubt.

In the end, the treaty was ratified by 20 to 10—the minimum two-thirds majority needed. The affair shattered the illusion of national political consensus and sullied the reputation of Washington, the nation's preeminent hero. But the principle of presidential control of foreign policy had been established, and for the moment Madison and his faction (soon to be known as Republicans) were outmaneuvered.

Jay's Treaty improved Anglo-American relations in a manner highly threatening to the Spanish government. Spanish diplomats interpreted the treaty as an Anglo-American alliance preparatory to a joint assault on Spanish Louisiana and Florida. As a result of these fears, Spain agreed in the Treaty of San Lorenzo (1795) to allow Americans free navigation of the Mississippi River and the privilege to deposit goods for export at New Orleans. This was crucial to western prosperity, given that few roads connected the trans-Appalachian west to the Atlantic coast. Spain also agreed in the treaty to withdraw its support from the various Indian tribes of the Southeast who were resisting the U.S. advance. By appealing to the interests and exploiting the fears of both Britain and Spain, the new national government had split them off from their Indian allies, allowing for major strides in securing the western frontier for American settlers.

"EMPIRE OF LIBERTY"

By 1800 the new national government had demonstrated an impressive capacity to impose its will at home and abroad. Indeed, for many, federal power was already too great, and ritualistic denunciations of centralized power already had become a staple of American political debate. Thomas Jefferson responded to this sentiment when he became president in 1801. In his inaugural address Jefferson pledged a "wise and frugal government," featuring tax cuts and a sharp reduction in the size of the military. Above all, he vowed a "strict construction," or narrow interpretation, of the powers granted to the government under the Constitution.

In light of this pledge to shrink the power of the federal government, it is especially ironic that Jefferson doubled the size of the nation's domain in 1803 by the purchase of the Louisiana territory from France. This bold stroke was prompted by fears that, once again, powerful European states aimed to "bottle up" the United States on the western frontier. This time Emperor Napoleon's secret reacquisition in 1801 of Louisiana from Spain (to whom it had been transferred in 1762 to avoid losing it to the British) meant that American access to the Mississippi River and New Orleans might be permanently closed. As Jefferson put it in a letter to American negotiator Robert Livingston: "The cession of Louisiana [to France] . . . works most sorely on the United States. . . . There is on the globe one single spot, the possessor of which is our natural and habitual enemy. It is New Orleans, through which the produce of three eighths of our territory must pass to market, and from its fertility it will ere long yield more than half of our whole produce and contain more than half our inhabitants." The gravity of the situation is seen in Jefferson's hinted willingness to ally the United States with Great Britain, if necessary, to remove the French from New Orleans.

Jefferson's first move was to send Livingston of New York and James Monroe of Virginia to Paris with an offer to buy New Orleans and the province of West Florida. To the shock and amazement of both men, Napoleon had decided to divest himself of the entire province of Louisiana in order to consolidate his forces in Europe and perhaps raise a New World rival to Great Britain. He instructed his brilliant diplomat Talleyrand to offer to the Americans all of Louisiana. The American diplomats accepted the offer almost on the spot, even though the move was unauthorized by their government and the territory to be purchased undefined in extent. Indeed, when Livingston inquired as to the limits of Louisiana, Talleyrand replied cryptically, "I can give you no direction. You have made a noble bargain for yourselves and I suppose you will make the most of it."

The purchase of Louisiana precipitated a constitutional controversy. The Constitution did not explicitly authorize the federal government to acquire new territories. Nor did it provide for the incorporation of peoples residing in those territories, in this case the more than fifty thousand Creoles of New Orleans in addition to untold numbers of Indians. Nonetheless Jefferson and most of the country embraced the expansionist thrust. The president envisioned the immense but essentially unexplored Louisiana region as "an empire for liberty," large enough to absorb the flood of Americans westward for many generations. He rationalized the dubious legality of his actions by invoking "the laws of necessity, of self-preservation, of saving our country when in danger."

Even as the country was adjusting to this massive expansion of its domain, the renewal of warfare between France and Britain in 1803 involved the United States more deeply than ever in European affairs. Once again American farmers and merchants presumed to profit from the wartime needs of the belligerents, and once again those belligerents planned to prevent the Americans from supplying the needs of their enemies. Napoleon's Continental System aimed to blockade the British Isles from all trade, including that of neutral states. In retaliation, Britain attempted to use its vast sea power to hinder Napoleon's access to foreign trade by seizing on the high seas any vessels bound for France or its allies. Even more outrageous was the practice of "impressment," by which British warships, faced with a chronic shortage of crewmen, would stop American merchantmen on the high seas and seize alleged deserters. Between 1804 and 1807 the British navy seized more than a thousand American merchant ships and the French about half that many.

In the face of these depredations the Jefferson administration continued to assert the right of Americans as neutrals to trade unhindered with belligerent powers. The idea was as audacious as when Tom Paine had first proposed it in *Common Sense* thirty years earlier. Yet by 1807 American prosperity had become intimately linked to getting American grain surpluses to foreign markets. In time the humiliation of ship seizures and impressment was tolerated by shipowners as an unavoidable cost of doing business.

The situation escalated when in 1807 five American seamen were seized off the American warship *Chesapeake,* which had been forcibly stopped within sight of the Virginia shoreline by the *HMS Leopard.* A great hue and cry arose for America's honor to be defended by a declaration of war—a prescription for disaster considering the nation's lack of military prepared-

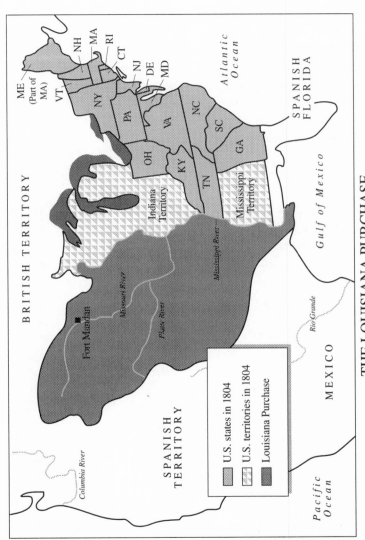

THE LOUISIANA PURCHASE

BRITISH TERRITORY

Atlantic Ocean

SPANISH FLORIDA

Gulf of Mexico

SPANISH TERRITORY

MEXICO

Pacific Ocean

Columbia River

Fort Mandian

Missouri River

Platte River

Mississippi River

Rio Grande

Indiana Territory

Mississippi Territory

ME (Part of MA)

NH
MA
RI
CT
VT
NJ
DE
MD
NY
PA
VA
NC
SC
GA
OH
KY
TN

U.S. states in 1804

U.S. territories in 1804

Louisiana Purchase

ness. Jefferson instead sought means of "peaceable coercion" to resolve the harassment of American vessels. In December 1807 he pushed through Congress an act declaring an embargo on all exports. No ships would be allowed to clear for any foreign port until France and Britain agreed to stop harassing American vessels. Jefferson believed that by cutting off the belligerents from essential foodstuffs and other supplies he could "peaceably coerce" them to comply with American policy.

The power to regulate commerce granted by the Constitution had now become the power to prohibit it completely. It was the most dramatic display of federal power to date. Unfortunately the effects of this new type of economic warfare fell most heavily upon American farmers, merchants, and shippers who saw their livelihoods destroyed almost overnight. Farm commodities accumulated and prices declined; cargoes began to rot at their wharves; economic distress pervaded the nation.

France and Britain, meanwhile, adapted to the embargo by imposing economies, seeking new sources of supply, and refusing to budge on the issue of neutral rights in wartime. Having failed to achieve its goals, the embargo was repealed in March 1809, to be followed by two equally ineffectual measures designed to compel respect for American principles and American trade. Efforts at "peaceable coercion" finally ended in 1811.

THE SECOND WAR OF INDEPENDENCE

A combination of militant western House members and weak presidential leadership led to a formal declaration of war against Great Britain in June 1812. Ostensibly fighting to defend the principles of neutral rights and national honor against the high-handed ways of Great Britain, the "expansionists of 1812" included the conquest of Canada and Florida as part of their war aims.

Shippers and merchants meanwhile found the immediate result to be the complete devastation of their interests. Whatever the outrages on the high seas, peace meant the continuation of business with their best customer. War changed that and prompted calls by many New Englanders for secession.

The Second War of Independence, more commonly known as the War of 1812, nearly destroyed the United States. Military operations against Florida and Canada soon bogged down, victims to lack of funds and often inept leadership. A British offensive in 1814 resulted in the burning of Washington, D.C. In 1815 a group of disgruntled Federalists met in Hartford, Connecticut, to discuss the possibility of seceding from the Union and perhaps reentering the British Empire.

Catastrophe was avoided only by Napoleon's defeat at Waterloo. With their main enemy trounced, the British were eager to resolve the annoying struggle with their erstwhile countrymen. On December 24, 1812, the "peace of Christmas Eve" ended the second war with Britain by reinstating the prewar status quo. The Treaty of Ghent resolved none of the causes of the war—impressment, neutral rights, "national honor." American negotiator John Quincy Adams remarked that "Nothing was adjusted, nothing was settled—nothing in substance but an indefinite suspension of hostilities was agreed to." Destruction of the Union had been averted. The condition of both the nation and its empire, however, remained precarious.

2

Hemispheric Supremacy

"Our country! In her intercourse with foreign nations may she always be in the right; but our country, right or wrong."—Commodore Stephen Decatur, 1816

A CURIOUS EXUBERANCE pervaded the country in the wake of the near-catastrophic War of 1812. Almost five thousand American lives had been lost, the nation's capital had been torched, and none of the war's objectives had been realized. National unity had been jeopardized and financial bankruptcy loomed. Yet politicians, newspaper editors, and veterans tended to appraise the conflict in favorable terms. Some took heart in the nation's ability to survive a second war with Great Britain. The military fiascoes in Canada and elsewhere were balanced by the splendid performance of the navy, which demonstrated an impressive capacity to go toe-to-toe with the mightiest navy in the world. And Andrew Jackson's magnificent victory at the Battle of New Orleans was the stuff of national legend. At the cost of only seventy of their own men, Jackson's army killed and wounded more than two thousand British troops. Who cared if the victory had occurred two weeks after the signing of the peace treaty on

Christmas Eve, before news of the treaty arrived? It appeared wondrous that in the face of military, political, and financial disaster, total defeat had somehow been avoided.

Although the war bitterly divided Americans, at the same time it served as a powerful stimulus to American nationalism, a means of national self-redefinition and reassertion. Former war hawk and now speaker of the House of Representatives, Henry Clay of Kentucky expressed satisfaction with the outcome: "A great object of the war has been attained in the firm establishment of the national character." In time of peril the survival and independence of the Republic had again been secured.

Along the same lines, many interpreted the struggle as a vindication of the collective manhood of the sons of the revolutionaries of 1776. For this generation a chronic sense of inadequacy as compared to their revolutionary fathers gave way to feelings of pride that their capacity for heroic action had not been dulled by material prosperity since the Revolution.

Still others saw the war as further proof of God's special relation to the American republic and as confirmation of its mission to regenerate the world. Congressman George M. Troup of Georgia remarked that at the Battle of New Orleans, "The God of Battles and Righteousness took part with the defenders of their country and the foe was scattered as chaff before the wind." Methodist preacher Joshua Hartt of Brooklyn sermonized: "It appears evident that God has been on our side. . . . If God be for us, who can stand against us?" In *A Scriptural View of the War* (1815), Reverend Alexander McLeod interpreted the war as a manifestation of "the Providence of God for extending the principle of representative democracy—the blessing of liberty, and the rights of self government." The Republic had been reborn.

No individual more personified the rising nationalist spirit than General Andrew Jackson, and no one's reputation more benefited from the war. Jackson's spectacular victories at New Orleans and at the Battle of Horseshoe Bend against the Creek Indians defined him as a mighty agent of American will. His backwoods persona and straightforward manner inspired respect and devotion; his periodic rages and unslakable desire for vengeance against his enemies inspired fear and awe. Even by 1817 he had achieved a certain a preeminence in the American political landscape as a spokesman for national unity and the rule of the "common man."

The mood of national reunion was fostered by the election in 1816 of James Monroe as president. Monroe's Virginia roots did not prevent him from reaching out to all sections and interests in the name of national reconciliation. A tour of the Middle Atlantic states, New England, and the upper West in the summer of 1817 by the new president (the first such tour since Washington) fueled the renewed sense of national unity and national consensus. The trip climaxed in Boston where Monroe addressed an enthusiastic crowd of forty thousand people. Amidst the bunting, flags, and toasting, the disaffection New Englanders felt toward the Union faded. Surveying the rising tide of harmony, a Boston newspaper reported an "era of good feelings" in American politics.

CRISES OF NATION AND EMPIRE

In spite of this exuberant mood, the nation faced formidable problems. The most pressing issue concerned the unsettled boundaries of the Louisiana territory. Spain had disputed the legality of the Louisiana sale from the start, claiming that the terms under which the province had been retroceded to France in 1801 prohibited its transfer to any other party without Spanish approval. For some years Spain had denied the

very legitimacy of the sale and presumed to reverse the trans-
action, though it received little support from the French in
these efforts.

By 1817 the Spanish government had reluctantly acknowledged the legitimacy of the sale of Louisiana to the United
States but hoped to define the province's ambiguous boundaries in the west at the Mississippi River—the same boundary
agreed upon by the 1783 Treaty of Paris. The Spanish also
claimed that the province of West Florida (that portion of the
present state west of the Perdido River) was not included in
the Louisiana Purchase, as claimed by the Americans.

The U.S. definition of Louisiana's boundaries had evolved
since 1803. Jefferson thought the "unquestioned" limits of
Louisiana to be those lands drained by the Mississippi and
Missouri rivers, bounded on the west by the Sabine River and
on the east by the Iberville River. These are the boundaries
depicted on today's schoolroom maps. But Jefferson insisted
that the United States had reasonable "pretensions" westward
as far as the Rio Grande River in the west and the Perdido
River to the east—in short, Texas and West Florida. By 1808
the implications of Lewis and Clark's discoveries prompted
Jefferson to include Oregon in the region encompassed by
Louisiana. Thus the maximum U.S. claim held that both
Texas and Oregon were included in the original deal with
France.

Whatever the scope of U.S. pretensions, Spain's determined
opposition challenged the Louisiana Purchase and threatened
navigation on the Mississippi. Jefferson's "empire of liberty,"
future home of America's rapidly multiplying millions and
safety valve of the Republic, stood dangerously unfinished.

The nation's imperial interests were challenged on the
southern border too, where the provinces of East and West
Florida remained outside America's grasp. Spain's continued

control of the Floridas impressed many as a dangerous anachronism. From the time of independence the Floridas seemed a natural appendage to the United States that was destined to be acquired at some point, a ripening fruit that would fall to the United States by a kind of political gravity.

The Floridas in Spanish hands were also perceived as a giant threat to the southern frontier. Its boundaries on a map led some to compare it to a pistol pointed directly at New Orleans. Louisiana could never be safe until the Gulf of Mexico had been made an American "lake." This was impossible as long as a foreign power controlled south Florida. Moreover, Spain's control of the Floridas limited access to the Gulf of Mexico via the Mobile and Apalachicola rivers, thereby hindering the economic growth of the lower South. In time of war the Floridas loomed as a near-impregnable fortress from which to invade the United States.

But perhaps the most pressing concern was that the Floridas in Spanish hands were a haven for runaway slaves and recalcitrant Indians, a base from which to launch border raids on Georgia settlements and then flee to safety. Large numbers of Creek Indians had fled into Florida in order to avoid attack, removal, or capture. The removal process had begun in the wake of the Creek War of 1812–1813. After annihilating Indian resistance at the Battle of Horseshoe Bend, Jackson had imposed on the Creeks the Treaty of Fort Jackson, which transferred 23 million acres to the United States. Although the treaty had been negotiated by Creek chiefs who had been allied with the United States during the war, Jackson justified the pact on the grounds that the entire Creek nation must be punished for the acts of those who had fought the United States. Creek chieftains who had resisted Jackson, including Francis the Prophet, escaped into Florida, where they joined with the Seminoles and bands of runaway slaves for mutual defense.

Equally alarming to many white Southerners was the existence of the "Negro Fort" on the Apalachicola River. Groups of runaway slaves had constructed the largest slave refuge in North American history from an abandoned British fort, complete with arms, gunpowder, and ammunition. The Negro Fort was destroyed in 1817 and more than 250 of its inhabitants killed when a cannonball from an American gunboat ignited the fort's powder magazine. Yet the province remained a place to escape the slave patrol and bloodhounds—an intolerable state of affairs to the slavemasters of Georgia.

The U.S. claim to the Floridas dated from the time of the Louisiana Purchase, when the American negotiator Robert Livingston claimed (incorrectly) that West Florida had been included in the agreement. In response to rising Spanish opposition to the Louisiana Purchase, Jefferson had vigorously asserted the claim to West Florida via the Mobile Act of 1804. This legislation called for a customs district to be established in West Florida as a visible symbol of federal authority. This provocative measure, designed to bully Spain into yielding, was withdrawn when it seemed likely to provoke war.

In 1811 Congress passed, in secret, the No Transfer Resolution. This landmark action asserted that, in view of its security interests along its southern border, the United States could not "without serious inquietude, see any part of the said territory pass into the hands of any foreign power"—in other words, the Floridas could not be transferred. The No Transfer Resolution authorized President Madison to seize East Florida and validated the annexation of a portion of West Florida by an ambitious party of American emigrants.

Annexation of the entire province seemed assured when American General George Matthews, using bribery to foment discontent, seized East Florida in March 1812. Yet the domestic and international outrage that greeted Matthews's brazen campaign forced the Madison administration to repudiate his efforts. East Florida was returned to Spain in 1813.

Efforts to wrest Florida from Spain were also complicated by the Latin American wars of independence. A series of revolts against three centuries of Spanish rule had broken out in the 1810s. By 1817 the success of the struggles remained uncertain, and many Americans, led by Henry Clay, called for some form of aid to the rebels, if only formal recognition of their revolutionary governments.

Spain, facing the dissolution of its empire, made it clear that it would break off talks on the southern boundary issue if the United States supported the revolutionary cause. Equally worrisome to U.S. leaders was the prospect that a concert of European powers (not including Britain), led by Russia and known as the Holy Allies, might launch an invasion of the Western Hemisphere to restore Spanish colonial authority. Thus American policy kept the Latin American revolutionaries at a distance.

The uncertain state of America's southern and western boundaries was matched on the north, where the border between Canada and the United States was ambiguously defined across almost its entire length. In the northeast, faulty geographic knowledge had created confusion over the Maine border stipulated in the Treaty of 1783. West of the Great Lakes, the northern boundary of Louisiana remained unclear, and a spirited naval arms race on the Lakes drained the resources of both sides. West of the Rocky Mountains, the United States vied with Great Britain for control of the

Northwest Coast, a region of vast extent and abundance for which Russia and Spain also contended.

American interest in the Northwest Coast dated from the voyages of Captain Robert Gray aboard the USS *Columbia*— the name that Gray bestowed on the river he explored in 1787. The reports of the explorer and adventurer John Ledyard, who had sent Jefferson tales of extensive fisheries and furs, further piqued American interest in the region as a zone of economic opportunity.

The fur magnate John Jacob Astor advanced American interests in the region in 1811 when his Pacific Fur Company founded the port of Astoria at the mouth of the Columbia River. During the War of 1812 Astor's agents sold Astoria to the British to prevent its capture. It remained in British hands despite the Treaty of Ghent's stipulation that all captured lands be returned. The increasingly lucrative fur trade encouraged British reluctance to concede the post, intensifying the imperial rivalry along the Northwest Coast.

Thus the northern, western, and southern boundaries of the U.S. imperial domain remained undefined. Negotiations between Secretary of State John Quincy Adams and Spanish minister Don Luis de Onis by late 1817 were again stalemated. Spain, relying upon the British to back its stand, obstinately resisted American demands. The crisis threatened the nation's security and its future.

Yet the nation's problems were not only external. Domestically the aftermath of the war had brought a period of general prosperity, but by 1817 a looming economic crisis threatened. The chief cause of this instability was a crippled currency. The War of 1812 had greatly increased national indebtedness. By 1816 devalued paper currency from dozens of state banks totaled an estimated $68 million. This had forced the federal government to take its revenues in these depreciated currencies, which often could be spent only in the state of issue. A rapid inflation resulted between 1815 and 1818, which both fueled economic growth and set the stage for collapse. The federal government had nearly gone bankrupt during the war. Only the last-minute purchase in 1814 of large quantities of government securities by merchant David Parish, financier Stephen Girard, and John Jacob Astor (at that time the richest individual in the country) had staved off catastrophe. In return for their financial assistance, Parish, Girard, and Astor benefited from the establishment of the Second Bank of the United States, which would stabilize the nation's currency and ensure that the government's securities would be repaid in full.

The creation of the Second Bank in 1816 introduced a measure of currency stability, but a steady outflow of the nation's silver reserves deprived the dollar of the hard-money backing it needed. Most of this silver was exported to China by a relatively few Northeastern merchants as a medium of exchange in the highly lucrative trade with Canton. This export of silver angered people in other parts of the country, and critics charged that a selfish monied elite was profiting at the expense of the nation at large.

Discontent over credit and currency matters thus took on a sectional flavor. Citizens of the trans-Appalachian West in particular and the South to a lesser extent perceived themselves to be in a quasi-colonial relation to the financial centers of the Northeast. Southerners shipped agricultural products north, often to be exported by Northeastern interests in exchange for manufactured goods and financial and transportation services. The Northeast sent manufactured goods to the West in exchange for foodstuffs and money. Poor or nonexistent roads also limited economic growth in the

West and South. The result was to center financial power in the Northeastern cities, especially New York, and to breed an ongoing fear and suspicion of the region by the South and West.

Currency problems and sectional economic rivalries paled in importance, however, compared to the problem of slavery. From the time of the Constitutional Convention slavery had been the deal breaker, the one issue that might make union impossible. Southerners made it clear they would enter no union that challenged the existence of the "peculiar institution." Compromise had made the Constitution possible; both Southerners and Northerners hoped that slavery would continue to diminish in profitability and gradually expire.

These hopes had been dashed by the invention of the cotton gin, which removed a major processing bottleneck and cleared the way for huge increases in production. Britain's textile revolution and the booming British demand for raw cotton it created ensured that slave labor would remain profitable for the foreseeable future. The year 1815 marked the beginning of the era of "King Cotton"; from 1820 to 1860 it was by far the nation's leading export. No one could deny that cotton and the slave labor that produced it were essential to national economic growth.

Yet by 1817 the persistence of slavery in the "land of the free" drove a wedge through pretensions of national unity. A sizable number of Americans were morally offended by human bondage, whatever they thought of blacks as human beings. Many more saw the institution as a social and economic threat that must not be allowed to spread into new states that might be carved out of the imperial domain. Almost all understood slavery to be the primary threat to the continued existence of the Union.

THE SEMINOLE WAR

After fifteen years of on-again off-again negotiations had failed to acquire the province of Florida, President Monroe and his secretary of war, John C. Calhoun, moved to accomplish the deed by military force. In late December 1817 American land and naval forces occupied Amelia Island on the Georgia-Florida border in order to root out a band of South American privateers whom the administration had labeled as pirates. Yet Monroe and Calhoun needed a dramatic incident in order to justify the course they contemplated—the conquest of Florida.

They got what they wanted as a result of lingering disagreement over the implementation of the Treaty of Fort Jackson. The Creeks who had escaped into Florida at the close of the Creek War had for some time challenged the legitimacy of the treaty by citing Article IX of the Treaty of Ghent, which guaranteed that lands lost by Britain's Indian allies during the war would be returned to them. British agents in Florida, Edward Nicholls and George Woodbine, encouraged this opinion by signing an agreement with the Creeks that their lands would be returned. In June 1815 the Madison administration instructed Andrew Jackson to begin to return the occupied territories.

But Jackson refused to comply with the presidential directive. President Madison, reluctant to anger Jackson's supporters, let the matter drop. The British, too, saw no reason to irritate the Americans by speaking out on behalf of their Indian allies. This opened the door for Jackson to employ bribery and intimidation to negotiate five more cessions of land between 1816 and 1818 from the Cherokee, Choctaw, and Chickasaw tribes. Yet many of the Creeks, together with their Seminole and free black allies, were unreconciled to being removed from their homelands.

Thus the Seminole War began as a consequence of the army's effort to implement the Treaty of Fort Jackson. A small band of Seminoles who had neither signed the treaty nor sided with the hostile Creeks refused the orders of General Edmund P. Gaines to vacate the village of Fowltown just north of the Florida-Georgia border. On November 21, 1817, Gaines and his troops stormed the village, killed several of its inhabitants, and burned Fowltown to the ground.

The Seminoles soon retaliated for this outrage. On November 30 they attacked a supply boat commanded by Lieutenant R. W. Scott as it ascended the Apalachicola River, killing most of its fifty passengers. The attack provided the administration with the pretext it needed. On December 16 Calhoun ordered Gaines to retaliate against the Seminoles, pursuing them into Florida if necessary. Ten days later Calhoun dispatched orders to Andrew Jackson in Nashville to proceed immediately to the Georgia-Florida border and assume Gaines's command. Aware of Jackson's capacity for aggressive action, Calhoun gave the general broad authority to pursue the Seminoles into Florida and "adopt the necessary measures to terminate" the Seminole raids. In instructions dated December 28, President Monroe was even more explicit: ". . . The movement against the Seminoles . . . will bring you on a theatre where you may possibly have other services to perform. Great interests are at issue. . . . This is not a time for repose . . . until our cause is carried triumphantly thro'."

Jackson had already seized the day. Upon hearing of the attack on the Scott party, he had called out his Tennessee volunteer militia and marched south. On January 6, 1818, before he had received his orders from Monroe and Calhoun, Jackson had written to the president that "the whole of East Florida ought to be seized and held as an indemnity for the outrages of Spain upon the property of our citizens.... This can be done without implicating the government; let it be signified to me through any channel ... that the possession of the Floridas would be desirable ... and in sixty days it will be accomplished."

By mid-March Jackson, at the head of almost three thousand Tennessee militiamen, American troops, and Indian allies, had descended the Apalachicola River deep into East Florida. His overwhelming force met minimal opposition from the vastly outnumbered Seminoles and Creeks. Hacking their way through the dense swamps, Jackson and his force torched the deserted Seminole villages of Miccosukee and Boleck's Town and destroyed the Indians' sources of food in a calculated attempt to inflict terror and starvation on the Seminoles. Jackson also captured the Spanish garrisons at St. Mark's and Pensacola, which offered little resistance to the American force.

Although Jackson was unable to engage the Indians in battle, he did capture several important enemy leaders. Creek chieftains Francis the Prophet and Himmilemmico were taken captive after being lured aboard an American naval vessel displaying a British flag. Francis, a charismatic spokesman for Indian unity, was a particularly valuable catch. Jackson had the Indian leaders summarily hanged as a fearsome warning to those who would challenge American power.

Jackson's men also captured Lieutenant Robert Christy Ambrister of the royal marines and Alexander Arbuthnot, a seventy-year-old Bahamian trader of Scotch descent. Jackson charged the two Britons with inciting the Seminoles and Creeks into making cross-border attacks on white settlements in Georgia. The two men made perfect scapegoats—"unprincipled villains," Jackson called them. The impromptu court-martial Jackson convened in Pensacola quickly condemned both men to death, though it then reconsidered and reduced Ambrister's penalty to fifty lashes of the whip. Jackson overrode the reconsideration, affirmed the death penalty against Arbuthnot, and had both men executed. Their deaths, he said, would function as "an awful example" to the Seminoles not to rely on British support or encouragement.

By late May Jackson had seized Pensacola, the capital of West Florida. The general alleged—incorrectly—that the garrison there sheltered four or five hundred Seminole warriors. Nonetheless Jackson was determined. Pensacola, he wrote, "must be occupied by American force." On May 24 Jackson's army seized the city, declared it a United States revenue district, and deported the Spanish governor and his soldiers to Cuba. The capture of both West and East Florida was complete. Jackson wrote to a confidant: "All I regret was that I had not stormed the works, captured the governor, put him on trial for the murder of Stokes and his family [American settlers killed by the Seminoles], and hung him for the deed."

While Jackson subjugated Florida, an incident occurred that was perhaps an inevitable consequence of the Indian-hating his campaign of terror and intimidation had wrought. Georgian militiamen commanded by Major Obed Wright, acting under orders of the state's governor, attacked and burned the Creek village of Chehaw. Wright's men slaughtered a dozen men, women, and children despite the fact that the villagers had actually fed Jackson's half-starved troops during the march south from Tennessee. Indeed, some of the men of the village were, at the time of the attack, serving under Jackson in Florida. Now their town was destroyed and their families murdered. A Georgia jury later found Wright innocent of any wrongdoing.

Jackson's heavy-handed tactics created a sensation in the national press. As reports of his movements slowly trickled north, few could believe that the Monroe administration had ordered such an audacious act of aggression against the territory of a European power. Both international law and constitutional precedent seemed to have been recklessly disregarded. Critics raised the possibility of a strong British reaction to the murder of two of its subjects and the naked conquest of the property of a sister monarchy. Spain reacted to events by immediately suspending negotiations with the United States and cultivating the support of other European powers. Surely this time the United States had overplayed its hand.

The scope of Jackson's audacious campaign startled Calhoun and Secretary of the Treasury William Crawford; they soon advised President Monroe to disavow Jackson's actions and return the captured territory. Both Calhoun and Crawford realized that the situation presented a prime opportunity to discredit a potentially formidable political rival. Yet Jackson's original orders had not explicitly prohibited the course he took, nor did the administration further clarify his instructions during the course of the campaign. Monroe, as secretary of war under James Madison, had disavowed the Matthews mission in 1812 when it had become a public embarrassment. Now, in the face of intense public criticism, he was inclined to do the same with Andrew Jackson.

Only the determined opposition of Secretary of State John Quincy Adams stood in the way of such a course. Adams had played no part in originating the Jackson mission, but he now understood that the resolution of the negotiations with Spain and perhaps the success of the Monroe administration depended on supporting Jackson's actions. Backing down now would remove the threat of force from the equation and thereby encourage Spanish intransigence at the bargaining table. The United States would appear weak and vacillating on the world stage—not the image a man with Adams's presidential aspirations wished to project. So Adams decried the plan to disavow Jackson as "weakness and a confession of weakness."

The force of Adams's argument eventually won over Monroe. Outright disavowal of Jackson might bring down on the White House the wrath of the general's huge public following. On July 20 Adams presented what he termed in his diary to be "a new point of view" on the matter: that Jackson had seized the Indian garrison at Pensacola in order to prevent its expulsion by the Spanish colonial governor. Adams privately acknowledged the absurdity of this view: "I admitted that it was necessary to carry the reasoning upon my principles to the utmost extent it would bear to come to this conclusion.—But if the question is dubious, it was better to err on the side of vigour than on the side of weakness—on the side of an officer who had rendered the most eminent service to his nation than on the side of our bitterest enemies." Adams realized that appeals to patriotism could overwhelm principled objections to Jackson's actions.

Monroe decided to defend Jackson and entrusted Adams with the task. What was needed was a public justification of Jackson, a vigorous defense against the charges that the administration had made war in defiance of constitutional procedure. Adams provided this justification in instructions sent in November 1818 to Minister to Spain George Erving in Madrid, and "leaked" to the press soon thereafter. Denying U.S. culpability for the Seminole War, Adams instead blamed Spain for failing to control the Indians of Florida. The origins of the Seminole War, Adams claimed, were to be found in the actions of the British provocateurs in the Floridas during the War of 1812. They had encouraged "all the runaway Negroes, all the savage Indians, all the pirates, and all the traitors to their country . . . to join their standard and wage an exterminating war" against the United States. Jackson had intervened in a "narrative of dark and complicated depravity" in which Spanish impotence and British agitation had incited the Indians against the United States.

Adams placed direct responsibility for the Seminole War on Alexander Arbuthnot, whom he described as "the firebrand by whose touch this negro-Indian war against our borders has been rekindled." Arbuthnot's "infernal instigations" that the Creeks were entitled to lands lost under the Treaty of Fort Jackson resulted in the "peaceful inhabitants" of Georgia being "visited with all the horrors of savage war." Jackson, Adams asserted, had merely punished the "mingled hordes of lawless Indians and Negroes" responsible for these outrages. Adams then justified the seizure of the Spanish forts "as necessary measures of self-defense."

Adams concluded his audacious communiqué with a vigorous defense of Jackson's actions: "The President will neither inflict punishment, nor pass censure upon General Jackson, for that conduct, the motives for which were founded in the purest patriotism." The Floridas would be returned this time, but Adams warned of the consequences of further Spanish "misconduct" in the Floridas: "If the necessities of self-defense should again compel the United States to take possession of the Spanish forts and places in Florida . . . another unconditional restoration of them must not be expected."

Adams's letter to Erving provoked a sensation when it was released in late December. It was one of the first great statements of Manifest Destiny. Jefferson, in retirement in Virginia, described the letter as being "among the ablest I have ever seen, both as to logic and style." Adams's biographer, Samuel Flagg Bemis, designated the Erving letter as Adams's "great gun" and asserted that it was "the greatest state paper of his career."

That Adams's letter to Erving fundamentally misrepresented the actual state of affairs was lost amid the patriotic upsurge generated by his defense of Jackson. These inaccuracies were publicly documented on February 24, 1818, in the report of a special Senate committee charged with investigating the Seminole War. The report disputed the administration's defense of the war and calmly asserted that Jackson had usurped the authority of Congress and the executive and inflicted "a wound on the national character."

But few Americans took much notice of these criticisms. Adams's bold defense of Jackson had shifted the focus from international law and constitutional scruple to a sacred narrative of American "right" versus Spanish, Indian, and British "wrong." Critics found themselves in the uneasy position of seeming to side with Spain against the nation's preeminent military hero.

A congressional investigation of Jackson paradoxically added to the general's popularity. After being cleared of any wrongdoing by Congress, Jackson embarked on a national tour during which he was mobbed by supporters. In Baltimore he told an adoring crowd, "What I have done was for my country." It was a critical moment in Jackson's life and in the life of the Republic: exposed to censure and disgrace, Jackson's career had been saved by Adams's determined stand on his behalf. The general emerged from the affair more popular than ever; he began to be seen as presidential timber.

Although Adams had formulated a response capable of dampening congressional and public criticism, would his argument satisfy opinion in Great Britain? The London press howled for vengeance for the slain British subjects, and opinion across Europe feared the self-aggrandizing tendencies of the Americans. So great was the outrage that the American minister in London, Richard Rush, observed that Britain's political leadership might have led the nation to war merely "by holding up a finger." Would the controversy lead to yet another conflict?

There was no chance that British Foreign Secretary Lord Castlereagh would allow things to come to that. In the aftermath of the War of 1812 cooler heads were beginning to prevail on both sides of the Atlantic. British leaders, particularly Castlereagh, fully appreciated that they stood to gain more from cooperation rather than conflict with their former colonies. Cotton exports were beginning their four-decade-long boom which would fuel English textile mills and Southern prosperity. Indeed, Anglo-American relations now began a long-term improvement that, with some setbacks, would carry into the twentieth century. Conflicts would still arise, but they would be managed, not exacerbated.

This diplomatic détente had its start almost imperceptibly in the signing of a commercial convention which reestablished trade in 1815. The trend accelerated with the signing of the Rush-Bagot Agreement of 1817 which demilitarized the Great Lakes. The agreement was one of the first and probably the most successful disarmament treaties in modern history, the first step in the creation of what eventually became the world's longest unfortified border.

By July 1818 Rush and veteran American diplomat Albert Gallatin were in London negotiating with their British counterparts the resolution of a number of unsettled issues. The talks produced the Convention of 1818 which demarcated the U.S.-Canadian border at the 49th parallel from the Lake of the Woods to the Rockies. The treaty also declared the vaguely defined Oregon territory west of the mountains to be "free and open" to both British and American settlement for a period of ten years. Ratified in December 1818, the convention with Great Britain cleared up critical ambiguities in the nation's northern border and strengthened the American claim to the Oregon territory.

The détente between the United States and Great Britain quashed Spain's hopes that the British would support them in talks with the Americans. Neither the pleas of the Spanish government nor the execution of two British subjects was about to derail the diplomatic reconciliation that was taking place between the United States and Great Britain. John Quincy Adams, whose learned mind was complemented by decades of experience as a diplomat, knew this and accordingly was not especially concerned that Britain might take offense at his indictment of British policy in the Floridas.

The Transcontinental Treaty

The United States' confrontational response to what at first had seemed a clear-cut case of reckless aggression startled the Spanish government. It was now obvious that the Monroe administration planned to seize the Floridas if negotiations were not soon concluded, and that the British would do nothing to prevent this from happening. Under duress, Spanish negotiator Don Luis de Onis returned to the bargaining table in late 1818 to make the best deal he could. The Floridas would have to be conceded to the United States. The sticking point now concerned their western boundary, where Spain still wished to deny the United States as much as it could of the Louisiana territory, including the province of Texas.

At this crucial stage in the talks, Adams and Monroe introduced a bold new demand: that the western boundary be extended along the still to be determined Mexican-American border, all the way to the Pacific Ocean. For the first time an American administration had laid claim to a "window on the Pacific." Heretofore American proposals had stopped at the front range of the Rocky Mountains. Now a major new diplomatic initiative had been broached, seemingly out of the blue.

In fact, American diplomacy had been moving toward a transcontinental claim since at least Jefferson's time. Lewis and Clark's journey had revealed the great river route west to Astoria, at the mouth of the Columbia River. The explorers had documented the rich bounty of furs in the Northwest, which it was envisioned could be exported to Asia as an ideal item of exchange for the China trade.

Astor's enterprise at the mouth of the Columbia River had further whetted the American appetite for the region. In 1817 Adams had ordered Commodore James Biddle, commanding the *USS Ontario,* to sail to Astoria and "to assert there the claim of sovereignty in the name of . . . the United States, by some symbolical or other appropriate mode of setting up a claim of national dominion." American access to the Northwest's furs could also reduce the export of silver to Asia, thereby bolstering the dollar. This bold move had startled the British but did not outrage them. They ratified the U.S. presence in the region by agreeing to the "free and open occupation" provision of the Convention of 1818.

It should be emphasized that official American interest in the Oregon territory first arose because of its potential as a neomercantile outpost in the international economic system. Only in the late 1830s and 1840s, after overhunting decimated the fur trade, did Oregon loom as a place for emigrant farmers.

In the negotiations with Spain, it was by no means clear

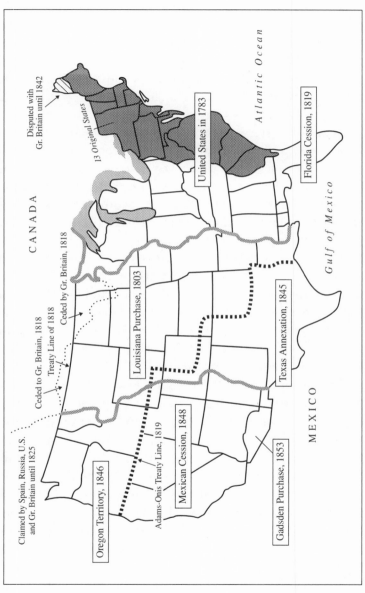

THE TRANSCONTINENTAL TREATY LINE, 1819

that Madrid would agree to this radical new proposal of a transcontinental boundary. It would require Spain to give up its tenuous claim to the Northwest Coast established by Juan de Fuca. To encourage the Spanish to do so, Monroe, with Adams's acquiescence, offered to exclude Texas from the American claim. In effect, a claim to Texas was given up in return for a claim to the Oregon country.

Monroe's correspondence leaves no doubt that the slave controversy and the threat its extension posed to the Union were the reason behind the move to exclude Texas. He wrote to Jefferson: "From this view, it is evident, that the further acquisition of territory, to the West and South, involves difficulties of an internal nature which menace the Union itself." Florida, presumably a future slave state, had been acquired. Controversy loomed over the admission of Missouri. Expanding the imperial domain to include Texas, at least at this point, was too much, too soon. At any rate, the claim that Texas was part of the Louisiana Purchase was dubious. Monroe and Adams agreed to barter this spurious claim in exchange for strengthening an equally spurious claim to Oregon. It was a decision with lasting consequences.

The agreement that Adams and Onis reached in February 1819 was met with near-unanimous approval. Although sometimes termed the Florida Treaty, its most significant long-term aspect concerned the establishment of a western boundary starting at the Sabine River, proceeding along the Red and Arkansas rivers north to the 42nd parallel, and from there to the Pacific (see map). The Transcontinental Treaty (as the pact would later be known) had far-reaching implications: the Louisiana Purchase had been not just perfected but expanded, and American interests extended into the Oregon country. Although diplomatic wrangling held up final ratification until 1821, negative responses to the treaty were muted.

Only later would the significance of the Texas cession be widely perceived.

In the courts of Europe the United States' sudden acquisition of both the Floridas and an expanded western domain caused concern. The Americans had taken another giant step toward becoming the preeminent New World empire. The British press characterized the treaty as further proof of the ambitious, aggressive, expansionist ways of their former colonies.

To Adams, however, the treaty was partial fulfillment of a divine plan: Europe, he wrote in his diary, must be "familiarized with the idea of considering our proper dominion to be the continent of North America." Expansion across the continent was "as much the law of nature . . . as that the Mississippi should flow to the sea. Until Europe shall find it a settled geographical element that the United States and North America are identical, any effort on our part to reason the world out of the belief that we are ambitious will have no other effect than to convince them that we add to our ambition hypocrisy."

THE MONROE DOCTRINE

Although the adroit use of force and diplomacy had produced for Monroe and Adams a spectacular victory in the confrontation with Spain, the threat of European intervention in the Latin American revolutions remained. Tsar Alexander I of Russia had by no means resigned himself to the destruction of a fellow monarch's colonial empire, and he labored intensely for a consensus among his "Holy Allies" that intervention in the New World was in the interest of conservative regimes across Europe. At diplomatic conferences at Troppau (1820–1821) and Verona (1822), Alexander overcame British opposition and secured allied military action to restore monarchy in Austria and in Spain, where King Ferdinand VII was rescued from house arrest at the hands of his republican adversaries and restored to full power. Monroe and Adams feared these developments as a prelude to intervention in the Western Hemisphere.

Yet these European efforts to reinstall reactionary regimes concerned the British as much as they did the Americans. Having gained access to the rapidly developing markets of South America as a consequence of the revolutionary upheaval, London did not wish to assist the reestablishment of a colonial regime whose first move likely would be to end British trading privileges. George Canning, who assumed the office of foreign secretary upon the suicide of Castlereagh in 1821, followed the ambiguous course charted by his predecessor—offering to assist Spain in a negotiated end to the struggles but flatly opposing armed intervention. Canning finally made British policy explicit in October 1823 during a conference with French minister Duke de Polignac, in which each side pledged not to intervene militarily in the South American rebellions.

Canning also looked to the United States to bolster Britain's position opposing European intervention. A joint Anglo-American declaration of principle, perhaps even a full-scale alliance, would guarantee the abstention of the other European powers in Western Hemisphere affairs. In this spirit Canning, in August 1823, approached American Minister Richard Rush with a startling offer: would the American government join the British in publicly declaring their mutual desire that the Latin American states remain free, independent, and not subject to transfer to any other European power? Would the Monroe administration consider making a statement publicly asserting this common position and mutually pledging that "We aim not at the possession of any portion of them ourselves"?

Canning's proposal created a sensation among American elite opinion. Aligning with Britain seemed to offer a way to guarantee that no further European (that is to say, non-British) intervention in the Western Hemisphere would occur. Both Monroe and former president James Madison were inclined to accept Britain's offer of a de facto alliance. Jefferson was enthusiastic about the possibilities. He advised Monroe that "By acceding to her [Britain's] proposition, we . . . bring her mighty weight into the scale of free government, and emancipate a continent at one stroke. . . . Great Britain is the nation which can do us the most harm of any one . . . and with her on our side we need not fear the whole world." The Americans seemed ready formally to ally themselves with their former mother country.

Once again, however, John Quincy Adams assessed matters from a more nuanced perspective. Ever suspicious of the British bearing gifts, Adams perceived that the real motive behind the offer was to induce the United States to renounce publicly further acquisitions of territory. What about Texas and Cuba, which might someday desire annexation to the Union? Adams argued to the other members of the cabinet that "we should at least keep ourselves free to act as emergencies may arise, and not tie ourselves down to any principle that might be brought to bear against ourselves. . . . It would be more candid, as well as more dignified," Adams contended, "to avow our principles explicitly to Russia and France, than to come in as a cockboat in the wake of the British man-of-war. . . . We should separate it from all European concerns, disclaim all intentions of interfering with these, and make the stand altogether for an American cause."

Adams recognized the essential fact of the matter: Canning,

through his actions and statements, had made Britain's opposition to European intervention unshakable. Therefore, why should the United States take part in a joint declaration by which it would gain nothing, and at the cost of a pledge of not to expand? With British policy certain and clear, Monroe and Adams were in a position "to avow [their] position explicitly to Russia and France" without making further commitments. The stage was now set for a formal declaration of these principles.

This occurred on December 2, 1823, in the president's seventh annual message to the Congress. The State of the Union address, as the annual message later became known, was an ideal vehicle for policy pronouncements to the public, to the European diplomatic corps, and to posterity. Buried amid the president's remarks on a range of issues were three paragraphs of profound long-term significance for both American and world history. The principles articulated, far from being primarily the result of cabinet infighting, as one historian has recently suggested, were in fact long aspired to by American political leaders. Only now were conditions favorable to their being raised to the level of holy writ, almost on a par with the Declaration of Independence.

The first of Monroe's principles was that of "noncolonization": ". . . the American continents, by the free and independent condition which they have assumed and maintain, are henceforth not to be considered as subjects for future colonization by any European powers. . . ." This bold prohibition on further colonization was bolstered by an equally vigorous statement against foreign intervention: "We owe it, therefore, to candor and amicable relations existing between the United States and those powers to declare that we should consider any attempt on their part to extend their system to any portion of this hemisphere as dangerous to our peace and safety. . . . It is impossible that the allied powers should extend their political system to any portion of either continent without endangering our peace and happiness. . . ." In effect, Monroe had defined the American security zone to include the entire Western Hemisphere. A justification was in place for future U.S. interventions throughout Latin America.

Having said, in effect, "Europe Hands Off!" the Western Hemisphere, Monroe assured European governments that the United States had no intention of intervening directly in the ongoing Greek struggle for independence from Turkey, in spite of widespread American ideological sympathy for the Greeks. By asserting the "doctrine of the two spheres," the third principle of his policy, Monroe declared the United States supreme in the Western Hemisphere while mollifying European concerns by pledging nonintervention in continental affairs.

In 1823 the United States was in no position unilaterally to enforce its candid statement prohibiting noncolonization and nonintervention. France and Russia, the parties at whom the statement was chiefly aimed, ridiculed the president's pronouncement. But the United States did not have to act alone to enforce its new foreign policy "doctrine": the British navy, as Adams had calculated, could be relied upon to repel any European threat. The United States could make its epochal policy statement without fear of its being contradicted by European actions, and without compromising its own future freedom of action.

The bold American statement had an inspirational effect on many South American patriot movements that interpreted Monroe's message as an offer of a pan-American alliance. Recognition of the South American independence movements had finally begun in 1822, and hopes arose that an era of hemispheric cooperation was dawning. Yet Adams and Monroe had no intention of multilateralizing their new policy. Don José Maria Salazar, the new Colombian minister to the United States, queried Adams on the implications of the president's remarks. Would the United States "enter into treaty of alliance with the Republic of Colombia to save America in general from the calamities of a despotic system"? Adams rejected the offer of alliance and assured Salazar the U.S. government would determine the timing and appropriateness of any collective response.

Most immediately affected by Monroe's new policy was Russia. Tsar Alexander had made his power felt in the Western Hemisphere in 1821 when he issued a ukase, or royal decree, claiming exclusive Russian control of the northwest American coast as far south as the 51st parallel, and prohibiting foreign vessels from approaching to within one hundred miles of the coast. Now, faced with the depletion of fur-bearing animals, the financial difficulties of the Russian-America Company (a fur-trading monopoly he had chartered in 1799), and mounting U.S. opposition to his ukase and to further Russian colonization, Alexander capitulated. In April 1824 Russia agreed to allow American vessels near-unrestricted access to the Northwest Coast and its adjoining waters.

For Adams and Monroe it was the capstone of eight years of brilliant diplomacy. In a precarious position in 1817, by 1824 the American nation and the American empire stood on firmer ground than ever before. From a position of relative insecurity the United States had emerged as the supreme power in the Western Hemisphere. The Louisiana Purchase had been perfected, the Floridas secured, a transcontinental claim had been staked, and the prospect of European intervention in the hemisphere greatly reduced. The age of Manifest Destiny had begun.

3

The Age of Manifest Destiny

"We are the nation of human progress. . . . "
—John L. O'Sullivan, 1839

BY 1826 THE UNITED STATES had established itself as a formidable power in its own right. Its vast dominion extended from Canada to the Gulf of Mexico and from the Atlantic Ocean to the Pacific via the Oregon country (see map). In the fifty years since independence, the thirteen fledgling British North American colonies had expanded into an empire larger than any European power, save Russia. The Mississippi River valley alone was larger than most European countries. The promise of unity—security, expansion, prosperity—had been fulfilled for all but the most optimistic Americans.

Approximately ten million Americans inhabited this vast domain—fewer than live in the New York City metropolitan area today. Most Americans still lived east of the Appalachian Mountains, well within the boundaries of the original thirteen colonies. Compared to almost any European state, the country was not overcrowded; yet the push for more and better land accelerated during the 1820s as pioneers, traders, and speculators pushed west and south along the watercourses west of the Appalachians in search of fertile territories, commercial opportunities, and speculative profits.

Americans anticipated the further expansion of their empire as the natural consequence of what had gone before. The possibilities seemed endless—further expansion across the North American continent, into Canada, and perhaps into Mexico, the Caribbean, and Central America as well seemed assured. One Kentuckian mused, "On the east we are bounded by the rising sun, on the north by the aurora borealis, on the west by the procession of the equinoxes, and on the south by the Day of Judgment."

By the 1820s the rapid growth and enormous success of the United States bred unbounded confidence in the future and in the nation. Events did seem to reveal a divine destiny in the American experience; the tide of world history appeared to be flowing in the American direction. The forces of popular government and the self-determination of peoples were gaining ground at home in the rise of Jacksonian democracy and in Europe, where a wave of republican revolutions stood poised to challenge the old regimes. It appeared to be America's sacred duty to expand across the North American continent, to reign supreme in the Western Hemisphere, and to serve as an example of the future to people everywhere. This was the Manifest Destiny of the American people.

Although the term Manifest Destiny did not achieve wide usage until the 1840s, the sentiments to which it refers arose in the aftermath of the War of 1812. John Quincy Adams's "great gun" in defending Jackson's invasion of Florida had been one of the first and most ringing declarations of Manifest Destiny. The document's zealous nationalism and emotional appeals in the face of contrary facts suggest the rhetorical foundations of the outlook. Manifest Destiny, in essence, was a philosophy to explain and justify expansionism both to Europeans, who viewed American aggrandizement with alarm, and to the American people themselves, who needed reassurance that the course was righteous. The rhetoric of Manifest Destiny varied according to sectional or partisan priorities, yet all its advocates presumed to define the meaning of America in ways that appealed to the heart as well as the head. Manifest Destiny was founded on the a priori conviction of the uniqueness of the American nation and the necessity of an American empire. It emerged from an ongoing discussion about the idea of America that took place in the press, the Congress, the public tavern, and even in the art and literature of the time.

Arguments expounding an American Manifest Destiny consistently reflected three key themes: the special virtues of the American people and their institutions; their mission to redeem and remake the world in the image of America; and the American destiny under God to accomplish this sublime task. Under the aegis of virtue, mission, and destiny evolved a powerful nationalist mythology that was virtually impossible to oppose and, for many, almost without an alternative.

Notions of America's special virtue had existed from the time of the Puritan settlements of the Massachusetts Bay Colony. John Winthrop's sermon in 1631, that the Puritan colony in Massachusetts Bay represented a "shining city upon a hill" from which the regeneration of the world might proceed, established an ideological foundation for grandiose pretensions. By the eighteenth century the European enlightenment had developed a view of America as a special place where human society might begin anew, uncorrupted by Old World institutions and ideas.

Beyond the virtues inherent in its institutions, the idea of America also hypothesized the special virtue of the American people. Jefferson gave voice to this sentiment in his *Notes on*

the State of Virginia (1787), when he described American
farmers as "the chosen people of God," a special breed of person in "whose breast he has made his peculiar deposit for substantial and genuine virtue." The fears of Jefferson and others
of the founding generation that urbanization, manufacturing,
and overindulgence in "luxuries" might corrupt the republican experiment gave way by the 1820s to an emerging sense
that America, with its democratic institutions and worship of
the "common man," could never be corrupted—provided it
could continue to expand.

This exaggerated sense of national virtue carried with it the
obligation that Americans had a mission to spread their way
of life to a world in desperate need of regeneration. Exactly
how this process was to occur remained contentious. Some
imagined the United States as a beacon to the world, spreading its idea by example. Others argued that the nation should
act as a lifeline, extending material and moral assistance to
foreign peoples (such as the South Americans) who were
struggling to establish republican government.

Few advocated that the United States should become directly involved in European controversies such as the Greek
struggle for independence. Nonentanglement in European affairs had been axiomatic since Washington's Farewell Address
in 1796. In 1821 John Quincy Adams framed the matter in
these terms: "America, with the same voice which spoke herself into existence as a nation, proclaimed to mankind the in-
extinguishable rights of human nature, and the only lawful
foundations of government. . . . But she goes not abroad, in
search of monsters to destroy. . . ."

Assumptions about America's special virtue and its presumed mission to regenerate the world rested upon a bedrock
faith that God had destined the United States for its special
role. The spread of republican government, Christianity, and

capitalism—the essence of America's regenerative blue-print—could have been entrusted only to a people specifically chosen by God for the task. Similar to notions of America's special virtue and mission, this sense of Americans as a "re-deemer nation" was first seen in the Puritans' belief that by coming to America they had established a covenant with God entrusting them with the regeneration of the Christian church.

For many Americans, notions of God's divine favor were fundamental aspects of their nationalism. John Quincy Adams's sense of himself and the nation as tools of a divine plan was the preeminent article of faith motivating his five decades of public service. The constitutional principle of sepa-ration of church and state may have prevented the establish-ment of an official religion, but this did not imply the separation of God and the American people, at least in the minds of many. As the religious revivalism of the Second Great Awakening burned over the country in the 1820s and 1830s, it fueled the assumption that a special providence watched over Americans to a degree that likely would have astounded the more rationalistic sensibilities of the Revolu-tionary era.

The nationalist dream of a Manifest Destiny did not in-clude nonwhite peoples. By the 1820s the idea and reality of American nationalism had entered a new phase. The univer-sal appeals of the Revolutionary era—liberty, justice, and equality for all the peoples of the world—had receded, to be replaced by an increasing sense of the special, superior charac-teristics of white Anglo-Saxon Americans. As the nineteenth century unfolded, American nationalism became defined in-creasingly in racial terms. The emerging concept of Ameri-cans as an Anglo-Saxon people combined with an increasing pessimism regarding the "improvability" of nonwhite peoples.

The prior faith that all could benefit from a healthy dose of American progress was replaced by a fatalistic belief in the inevitable demise of what were presumed to be inferior groups. Blacks, Indians, and Mexicans in particular were by the 1830s most often seen as obstacles to progress, incapable of improvement.

In short, by the 1820s the American people had placed themselves at the center of a nationalistic narrative of their own creation. They perceived themselves as agents of God's will, destined to redeem the world and not inclined to compromise with those who disagreed.

THE GOSPEL OF COMMERCE

Americans spread their gospels of progress and regeneration to the world chiefly via the mechanism of commerce. Self-righteously rejecting the expansion of their dominion by the sword (even as the sword was at times employed for this purpose), Americans from all levels of society embraced the commercial potential offered by the nation's vast natural resources and fluid social structure. Commercial exchange was at the center of the American way of life. As early as 1800, New York Congressman Samuel L. Mitchill had observed that "The voice of the people and their government is loud and unanimous for commerce. . . . From one end of the continent to the other, the universal roar is Commerce! Commerce! Commerce!"

Many understood commerce to be, as John Quincy Adams put it, "among the natural rights and duties of men." Commercial exchange not only provided material rewards, it bound people together in the terms Americans understood best: self-interest. Henry Clay captured the fervor when he described commerce as "a passion as unconquerable as any with which nature has endowed us. You may attempt to regulate—you cannot destroy it."

Private enterprise defined America's relations with foreign civilizations. An eruption of entrepreneurial power throughout the world beginning in the 1780s gained speed in the nineteenth century and served as a great engine in the creation of a global marketplace. Like filings to a magnet, American entrepreneurs moved toward profit opportunities wherever they might be found. American trade, American technology, and American expertise began to penetrate all corners of the globe, bringing with them an inevitable modernization of the societies they contacted. American merchants and entrepreneurs vigorously exported not just their wares but a way of life that was reflexively conceived of as rational, modern, and irresistible to all whom it touched.

By the 1820s American overseas commerce was part of a global trading network centered on the North Atlantic but with important interests in the Mediterranean, the Pacific, and South America. Even then it was obvious that the United States occupied a strategic position in the emerging world economy, and Yankee traders moved to make the most of those advantages.

By far the most important commercial tie was with Great Britain. By 1820 relations between the two countries were cemented by bonds of economic interest that no longer could be upset by politico-ideological squabbling. The cotton trade dominated this relationship. Between 1820 and 1860 cotton comprised approximately 60 percent of the value of all American exports, and most of these went to Great Britain.

This expanding trade relationship drew the United States into the British economic orbit. Between 1815 and 1850 the fluctuating British demand for American agricultural goods and raw materials directly affected U.S. prosperity. Large

trade deficits, caused by an insatiable demand for British manufactured goods and a slackening desire for American agricultural products, characterized the trade relationship. The
export of large quantities of specie from East Coast banks,
with their accompanying national credit contractions, could
precipitate economic downturns, as occurred in the depression
of 1819 and the panic of 1837.

In addition to the direct trade relationship, U.S. economic
development was closely linked to the English economy via
the Baring Brothers banking firm. Baring's, sometimes
known as the "sixth power of Europe," facilitated American
monetary exchanges abroad and funneled large sums of
British investment capital into the United States that proved
crucial to national development.

While considerably less extensive than the British connection, the United States also had important trade ties with
France and other European countries. Even Russia had important commercial links to the American republic. In the
1830s U.S. ships carried the bulk of Russian sugar imports
from the British West Indies, and Americans assisted in the
construction of the first steam vessel in the Russian navy.
In the 1840s the American engineer George Washington
Whistler supervised construction of the first Russian railroad,
and Americans provided technical assistance in the building
of the first Russian telegraph.

The size and significance of the commercial connection
with Northern Europe did not diminish the importance of
U.S. trade ties with other regions. In the Pacific, American interests were guided by a steady and persistent push for access
to the China trade. Interest in Asian markets first arose in
1784 when the merchant vessel *Empress of China* returned to
New York from Canton with a modest profit and immodest
expectations about the potential of the China market. Al-

though vast distances and hazardous conditions made travel to Asia difficult, the promise of windfall profits on a cargo of exotic goods excited the New York and New England mercantile elite. Over the coming decades this trade spawned many American fortunes in spite of the Chinese view of the foreigners as hairy, foul-smelling "barbarians" and their insistence that trade be conducted solely on their terms.

The emergence of the whaling industry also drew Americans into the Pacific. The demand for whale oil for lamps and lubrication exploded during the first decades of the nineteenth century. Even after petroleum began to replace whale oil, the hunt continued for items such as baleen, a flexible yet sturdy type of whalebone used for items such as umbrella frames and corset stays. Americans dominated the industry—at the peak of the whaling era, between 1835 and 1855, American vessels comprised about 80 percent of the world's whaling fleet.

While whalers roamed the length and breadth of the Pacific, Hawaii functioned as the crucial way station between the southern and northern Pacific hunting grounds. The year 1820 marked the arrival of the first American whaling ship in Honolulu. Even then the importance of the Hawaiian Islands as a source of sandalwood (an aromatic wood craved by the Chinese) and as a critical juncture in the central Pacific was obvious. By the 1840s the islands were becoming an important source of sugar for the American mainland and an incredibly lucrative source of wealth for shrewd and at times unscrupulous operators.

The rising strategic importance of Hawaii prompted the United States to oppose the control of the islands by any other country, particularly the French or British. In 1842 Secretary of State Daniel Webster decreed that "The United States . . . are more interested in the fate of the islands and of their government than any other nation can be; and this consideration induces the President to declare . . . that the Government of the Sandwich Islands [Hawaii's former name] ought to be respected; that no power ought either to take possession of the islands as a conquest, or for the purpose of colonization, and that no power ought to seek for any undue control of the existing Government, or any exclusive privileges in matters of commerce."

Webster had in effect invoked the Monroe Doctrine on territories more than three thousand miles away from any U.S. soil. In 1849 Secretary of State John M. Clayton declared that "The U.S. do [sic] not want the islands, but will not permit any other nation to have them."

Elsewhere in Asia, U.S. economic interests manifested themselves in places such as Sumatra, where companies based in Salem, Massachusetts, dominated the world pepper trade, and Mocha, a town on the Red Sea that served as a key source of coffee. Americans brought ivory from Zanzibar, and from Smyrna Turkish opium, which played a key role in the never-ending search for something other than silver to exchange with the Chinese.

THE MISSIONARY FRONTIER

No description of the U.S. presence in the world in the early nineteenth century would be complete without attention to the prominent role of missionaries in spreading the gospels of Christianity, commerce, and American notions of progress. Much like American nationalism, American evangelical Christianity was a philosophy that needed to be spread abroad as a way of bolstering its vitality at home.

The beginning of the American Christian missionary movement is reputed to have occurred in 1806 when S. J. Mills, a freshman at Williams College in Massachusetts, while

hiding in a haystack from a thunderstorm, experienced a revelation to spread the gospel to all the world. Six years later Mills
and four colleagues were the first American missionaries to
depart for foreign shores, under the aegis of the recently
formed American Board of Commissioners for Foreign Missions, a Congregationalist body. Not long thereafter the
American Baptist Missionary Union was formed to send its
emissaries abroad, the first of many sects that would follow
the Congregationalists' lead. The missionary movement had
begun.

The broader sources of the American missionary movement are to be found in the upheavals of the Second Great
Awakening, or Great Revival, which reached its peak in
the 1820s. Amidst the atheism of the French Revolution, the
ultra-rationalism of the Enlightenment, and the relentless
assault upon tradition that characterized the birth of the modern world, the Awakeners preached of good old-fashioned
fire, brimstone, and damnation. Yet they added a modern
twist: unlike the Puritan forefathers, the Awakeners placed
responsibility for salvation squarely upon the back of the
individual. Life was no longer "predestined"—now individuals chose heaven or hell, based upon the choices they made in
life. This new autonomy for the spiritual being proved the
perfect complement to the new autonomy of the economic
being that so greatly defined the modern American. Free
wills, free markets, and free men seemed to be the wave of the
future.

The missionary movement was given special urgency by
the widespread perception that the end of the world was near,
and that a millennium or Golden Age before the Second
Coming of Christ was within sight. This view found evident
support in the very existence of the United States—a society
at once so new, so hitherto unknown to human society, that it

was often presumed to be a revelation of a godly plan. American missionaries usually were patriotic nationalists of a high order, combining a secular vision for the political regeneration of the world with a spiritual vision of rebirth.

Close reading of the Scriptures seemed to suggest that the millennium would begin in the year 1866 A.D.— thus making all the more feverish the efforts to gather souls to Christ in the brief time that remained. Redemption from earthly misery would come by adopting a way of life remarkably similar to that presently being evolved in the United States. Ardent zeal came to characterize both the American missionary and the American nationalist, often one and the same person.

The 1820s, 1830s, and 1840s saw missionary enterprises in, among other places, Greece, Turkey, Persia, Constantinople, India, Ceylon, China, and Hawaii. Wherever they went, American missionaries took with them a printing press for spreading the word of God and a commitment to educate the heathen so that they could read it. In Hawaii the missionary presence was felt beginning in 1820 when a group of Congregationalists led by Hiram Bingham of Massachusetts commenced to save the native population from its habits of polygamy, unabashed sexuality, and pagan worship. The reluctance of the population at large to embrace the stern doctrines of evangelical Christianity precipitated a strategy of converting the Hawaiian tribal leaders under the not unreasonable expectation that their flock would then follow.

For the Hawaiians, exposure to the piety of the missionaries, the greed of the whalers, and the deadliness of the microbes that they and other visitors brought with them combined to reduce the native population from an estimated 300,000 when Europeans first arrived in 1778 to fewer than 50,000 a century later. By the 1850s Chinese "coolie" labor was being imported to work in the sugar cane fields, and Hawaiians soon became a minority in their own land.

FEDERAL SUPPORT FOR OVERSEAS COMMERCE

While private citizens conducted the bulk of U.S. affairs with the world via their commercial enterprises, their endeavors were given indispensable support during the period 1815–1860 by the federal government. Presidential administrations from Monroe to Buchanan linked the nation's security to its economic well-being and, with considerable long-term consistency, crafted policies designed to support American commercial expansion and American principles of international law and commerce. Commercial expansionism was both an ideological imperative and an economic necessity, a means to Americanize the world as well as stimulate the internal development of the United States. American political leaders usually considered the expansion of commerce to be virtually synonymous with the promotion and defense of American nationalism, though the direction of that expansion was often subject to intense debate.

Exports were essential to American economic well-being. The profits gained by overseas trade were the difference between prosperity and stagnation. American exports rose almost continuously during the period 1815–1861, increasing from $178 million to $252 million during the period 1851–1854 alone. Between the early 1820s and the late 1850s, cotton exports rose from an average of $25 million to $150 million per year; foodstuff exports from an average of $11 million to $55 million; and manufacturing exports from an average of $5.5 million to $33.5 million.

Federal support for foreign trade expansion was based on

the assumption that the nation's prosperity depended on finding new markets for America's productive surplus, if only to reduce the reliance on Great Britain and France. At the same time American political leaders understood that the development of an overseas commerce was integrally linked to the construction of a national political and economic union. They provided vigorous and consistent support for private overseas commercial ventures by negotiating commercial reciprocity treaties with foreign governments, actively supporting a broad definition of neutral rights, staunchly advocating the principle of freedom of the seas, aggressively attempting to recover damage claims made by American citizens against foreign governments, and expanding the consular service to facilitate American business overseas. These policies, pursued with varying degrees of energy and success, provided crucial support for an American shipping industry that by the 1830s boasted the second largest carrying trade in the world.

Federal policy proved especially helpful to Americans doing business in China. As trade with China rose steadily in value and volume, American merchants pressured the U.S. government to negotiate a treaty of commerce with the Chinese. In 1842 Secretary of State Daniel Webster, keenly attentive to the needs of many China merchants from his home state of Massachusetts, received from Congress monies to appoint a commissioner to China empowered to negotiate a trade treaty based on the most-favored-nation principle. Webster selected Caleb Cushing, son of one of Boston's wealthiest merchants, to persuade the Chinese that the Americans, unlike the other European powers in China, did not seek colonies in Asia.

By the time Cushing arrived in Canton in 1844, trade restrictions had already eased as a result of the Opium War of 1839–1842. British gunboats had bombed the Chinese into submission; they now relaxed the terms of trade to all foreigners, including Americans, thereby making Cushing's mission less important than before. Nonetheless the Treaty of Wanghia (July 1844) opened four new ports to American traders, gained most-favored-nation status for the United States, and, most important, established the principle of extra-territoriality, by which Americans accused of crimes in China would be tried by an American consular official according to American law.

In what has been called "hitchhiking imperialism," the United States capitalized on the advantages gained by British aggression against China without having to take part in the hostilities. The Treaty of Tientsin (1858), extracted amid the chaos of the Taiping Rebellion, expanded the opportunities and privileges afforded to Americans by the Treaty of Wanghia as well as protecting the lives and property of American missionaries in China. In the years before the Civil War, Americans played a major role in the China trade and fought for equal access to its markets—what later would be known as the "open door" policy.

THE ROLE OF THE NAVY AND THE ARMY

The United States Navy lent invaluable assistance to America's burgeoning overseas commercial interests. In spite of its limited force, the navy was dispatched globally to defend the rights and interests of American citizens, to assist in the negotiation of trade treaties, to engage in exploration and hydrographic research, and to punish alleged violators of American rights and honor. By the 1850s the navy played an important and expanding role in the rapidly growing American commercial empire.

The Jackson administration's interest in aiding the development of American overseas commerce was demonstrated by the missions of Edmund Roberts to Asia in 1832–1834 and 1835–1836. Roberts was a New Hampshire native whose travels and tradings had taken him to much of the known world. His glowing tales of markets to be opened and riches to be reaped prompted Jackson to dispatch Roberts aboard the *USS Peacock* on a tour of Asia as an emissary of the young American republic. En route Roberts became one of the first Americans to visit Cochin China (later known as Vietnam), though he failed to gain a commercial treaty from the Vietnamese. While in Thailand, Roberts was feted as royalty and departed from the Kingdom of Siam with an agreement guaranteeing Americans commercial access equal to the British and French. Roberts also succeeded in securing a commercial treaty with the sultan of Muscat, on the east coast of Africa.

Yet Roberts failed at the most important part of his mission—opening the markets of Japan. Still the "hermit kingdom," the Japanese refused to have more than minimal contact with the outside world. Roberts judged that his rapidly dwindling supply of presents and lack of naval firepower rendered him ill-equipped to sail into Tokyo, and instead he returned to the United States to lobby for a second mission to Japan. Unfortunately Roberts's second mission also failed. Before arriving in Japan he contracted cholera and died in June 1836. The "opening" of Japan to the world would have to await the more energetic methods of Matthew C. Perry. Nonetheless, the largely forgotten missions of Edmund Roberts form a milestone in U.S. relations with East Asia. In the aftermath of Roberts's work, U.S. consuls were stationed in Singapore, Capetown in southern Africa, Zanzibar, and Muscat. The commercial potential of Asia had been probed and was found to be encouraging.

The navy's critical role in assisting the development of U.S.

overseas commerce was most spectacularly seen in what was officially known as the United States South Seas Exploring Expedition—more commonly called the Wilkes Expedition, after its commander Charles Wilkes. The mission was conceived as a way to test the "Holes in the Poles" theory of John Cleve Symmes of Ohio. Symmes had gained wide publicity for his crackpot idea that the interior of the earth was hollow and could be entered by openings at either pole. New England whaling and sealing interests, eager for more knowledge of the world's little-known regions, adopted Symmes's cause and persuaded Congress to finance a mission of exploration unprecedented in its scope. Between 1838 and 1842 Wilkes and his fleet of six (later five) naval vessels sailed over 90,000 miles, surveyed 280 islands, made 180 charts of various regions of the Pacific Ocean, and surveyed 800 miles of the Oregon coast and over 1,500 miles of the coast of Antarctica. Wilkes's extensive collection of native artifacts from the many indigenous peoples he met during his journey formed the basis of the Smithsonian Institution's original holdings and represented one of the first contributions to the science of anthropology.

Wilkes also assumed the mantle of avenger of American rights far from home. While in the Fiji Islands, his investigation of the murders of ten American ship members in 1834 led to the capture of a Fiji leader named Vendovi for the crime. Vendovi remained a prisoner on board Wilkes's flagship, the *Vincennes,* for two years, dying shortly after finally arriving in New York. Later the murder of two American officers by Fijians led to retaliatory raids that left more than eighty natives dead. Wilkes did his best to demonstrate, as one of his men put it in a letter home, "that to kill a white man was the very worst thing a Feegee man could do."

The navy had been deployed to defend American commerce and rights globally since the undeclared wars against the Barbary pirates of 1803–1805. One of the most dramatic displays of its role occurred in 1832 in the West Sumatran port of Quallah Battoo. During the first three decades of the nineteenth century, hundreds of American vessels traveled to Sumatra in search of pepper. While Sumatra was nominally a Dutch colony, the Dutch proved unable to evict the American pepper traders who came to control the world market in that spice. This trade proved quite profitable to both Americans and native Malays until the collapse of the world price for pepper in 1831 created hard feelings all around. In February 1831 a gang of Malays attacked crew members of the merchant ship *Friendship* of Salem, Massachusetts, killing two and stealing more than $20,000 in specie, opium, and supplies.

When word of the incident reached Washington, outraged American shipowners demanded action. In response to their entreaties, President Andrew Jackson dispatched the fifty-gun navy frigate *Potomac* to Quallah Battoo to secure restitution for the theft and punishment of the perpetrators. After a cursory attempt at negotiation, on February 6, 1832, commanding officer Captain John Downes and 260 marines launched a predawn assault on Quallah Battoo. The ensuing struggle left more that 200 Malay men, women, and children dead, at the cost of two marines dead and seven wounded. Unable to find either the stolen goods or those involved in the crime, Downes torched Quallah Battoo. The next day the *Potomac*'s guns shelled the remnants of the smoldering town for ninety minutes in a further effort to secure justice. Although he never found the stolen goods or the murderers, Downes finally agreed to depart after receiving numerous assurances that the *Friendship* incident would not be repeated.

News of Captain Downes's action startled the country. An assault on a foreign country resulting in the deaths of hundreds of innocent civilians offended both humanitarian and constitutional principles, and some of Jackson's political enemies sought to make an issue of the affair for the 1832 election. Yet in the end no punitive action was taken against either Downes or Jackson. The assault on Quallah Battoo came to be remembered, as one historian put it, "as a necessary lesson to be taught ignorant savages who would violate the rights of a young republic with a world destiny to fulfill."

In the long run, the navy's most significant expedition during this period was Commodore Matthew C. Perry's mission to "open" Japan to American commerce. At the urging of New England whaling and other commercial interests, Congress allocated funds for a naval expedition aimed at ending the "hermit kingdom's" two centuries of self-imposed isolation by demanding that Japan open its markets to American goods, guarantee the safety of American castaways, and provide coaling stations for the nation's rapidly expanding ocean-going steamship fleet.

President Millard Fillmore justified the mission in his December 1852 annual message to Congress. The nation's recently acquired "settlements on the Pacific," he noted, had stimulated "a direct and rapidly increasing intercourse" with East Asia. Citing the need for coaling stations and aid to shipwrecked sailors, Fillmore also called for the establishment of "mutually beneficial" commercial ties with Japan, though he disclaimed any intention of acquiring formal colonies so far from America's shores.

Then Fillmore offered a more theoretical rationale for the mission: "We live in an age of progress, and ours is emphatically a country of progress. . . . The genius of one American has enabled our commerce to move against the wind and tide and that of another has annihilated distance in the transmission of intelligence. . . . Whatever may be the cause of this unparalleled growth in population, intelligence, and wealth, one thing is clear—that the government must keep pace with the progress of the people."

Perry, commander of the navy's East Asia Squadron, relative of War of 1812 naval hero Oliver Hazard Perry, and himself an ardent expansionist, was selected to lead the mission to Japan. In 1852 Perry wrote, "Our people must naturally be drawn into the contest for empire," and he now committed himself to compelling the Japanese to submit to his will in order to expand the American foothold in Asia. On the morning of July 14, 1853, Perry's fleet of four warships arrived in Tokyo Bay. The belching black smoke from his steam-powered vessels amazed and terrified the Japanese, who had never seen such technology. Accompanied by four hundred heavily armed troops and a brass band playing "Hail, Columbia!," Perry came ashore and delivered an official letter from President Fillmore demanding that Japan open its gates to the world.

Gently turned aside by the Japanese, Perry withdrew his force only to return the following February with a fleet of nine warships. Awed by the American's power, the Japanese agreed to meet with him to exchange gifts. Perry later remarked that the American present of a quarter-scale railroad train set and telegraph system was of far greater value than the numerous art objects offered by the Japanese. In any case, the Japanese consented to guarantee the safety of castaways, provide the Americans with two coaling ports, and establish a consular office. But they refused to open their markets to the United States. That would not occur until American consul Townsend J. Harris secured full diplomatic ties and a formal commercial treaty in 1858.

Lieutenant John Rodgers's Northern Pacific surveying expedition of 1853–1856 broadened the trail blazed by Perry.

Rodgers and his small squadron extensively surveyed portions of the coastlines of China, Russia, and Japan. Rodgers understood that his mission was to "survey the particular fields of our commercial enterprise. Our ships from San Francisco to China and our whalers in the Pacific . . . whiten the ocean. For them, if I judge rightly, was this expedition fitted out." The United States on its way to becoming a power in Asia. Perry later predicted that "the people of America will, in some form or another, extend their dominion and their power, until they shall have brought within their mighty embrace the Islands of the Great Pacific, and place the Saxon race upon the eastern shores of Asia."

While the navy performed a key service to the American commercial empire by its exploration and mapping of the world's oceans and its dispensation of rough justice, the U.S. army played an essential role in the development of a continental empire, primarily through its Corps of Topographical Engineers. Originally the surveying unit of the Continental Army, the corps was formally created by the Army Reorganization Act of 1838. Under the leadership of Colonel J. J. Abert, the corps, in the words of its chronicler William Goetzmann, "functioned as a central institution of the era of Manifest Destiny, reflecting its problems and achievements."

The Corps of Topographical Engineers assumed substantial responsibility for sorting out and inventorying the vast domain acquired during the age of Manifest Destiny. Its small cadre of officers, scientists, and enlisted men explored trails, mapped mountains, supervised road construction, assessed natural resources, prospected for minerals and water, charted rivers, surveyed harbors, built dams, and laid out coastal fortifications. The corps's federally subsidized operations were indispensable to the economic development of the West, performing tasks that the private sector could not. Goetzmann assesses the legacy of the corps in the West as "more than any-thing else, a picture of the cultural mind in action. . . . Above all, it provides a picture of man employing all of his skills to arrive at a kind of ordered knowledge of his environment." Yet the Corps of Topographical Engineers did more than merely survey and catalogue the West. As the age of Manifest Destiny unfolded, the corps and its officers became increasingly politicized on behalf of expansionist interests. Perhaps the most famous example of this were the exploits of John C. Frémont. Son-in-law to Missouri Senator Thomas Hart Benton, Frémont shared Benton's enthusiasm for Western expansion and national aggrandizement. With Benton's encouragement and sponsorship, Frémont embarked in 1842–1845 on three reconnaissances designed to strengthen the U.S. claim to the far West by securing greater knowledge of the region. While Frémont's voyages ultimately did little to add to the store of scientific data, they did much to publicize the wonders of the little-known lands of the West beyond the Rocky Mountains. Frémont capped his career as an "explorer" by leading the "Bear Flag Revolt" of 1846 in California, a prelude to the province's annexation by the United States in 1848.

INDIAN REMOVAL

Perhaps no one development epitomized the motives and contradictions of Manifest Destiny more then the forced removal of approximately 125,000 Indians who still inhabited the lands of the Southeast. The massive and expanding demand for raw cotton was directly responsible for the urgency attached to removing Indians from fertile lands in what soon became the plantation South. Indian relocation was driven by private greed, justified by appeals to scripture and civilization, and accomplished, at a fearsome cost in human misery, by the federal government.

The final defeat of Indian resistance in the Southeast by 1815 had left the remaining tribes confined by treaty to parcels of land a fraction the size of their original holdings. Nonetheless, as the global demand for cotton exploded in the 1820s, frontier speculators and entrepreneurs covetously eyed Indian lands in Georgia, Alabama, Mississippi, Louisiana, and Tennessee as prime territory for the expansion of cotton production. The era of "King Cotton" had begun, the plantation myth of the Old South was about to be acted out, and the Southern ruling elites began to evolve an unshakable faith in their own importance to both national and global economic development. Realization of this grandiose vision, however, required the removal of the current inhabitants of these lands.

The legal status of the subjugated tribes had long been uncertain—were they independent nations, wards of the American state, or some combination of the two? In 1830 Chief Justice John Marshall of the U.S. Supreme Court deemed them to be "domestic dependent nations" who retained some autonomy even as they were subordinated to the will of the federal government. Marshall also upheld the principle of Indian treaty rights and argued that the tribes could not be dispossessed of their land without due process of law.

Yet the rapacious speculators and frontiersmen of the Southern frontier would tolerate no discussion of the treaty rights of Indians or of their human rights in any form. Indian domains posed a barrier to the untrammeled pursuit of the wealth of the land. Thus Governor George Gilmer of Georgia proclaimed that "Treaties were expedients by which the ignorant, intractable, and savage people were induced without bloodshed to yield up what civilized people had a right to possess by virtue of that command of the Creator delivered to man upon his formation—be fruitful, multiply, and replenish the earth, and subdue it." Sentiments such as these, in the country at large and within the Democratic party in particular, fueled demands for Indian removal.

When Georgia moved to defy Justice Marshall's ruling by allowing removal to proceed, a direct threat to federal authority seemed at hand. But President Andrew Jackson, the people's choice and himself the premier champion of Indian removal, chose to ignore the implications of Justice Marshall's ruling. "The Supreme Court has made their ruling," he reputedly said. "Now let them enforce it." Jackson's passivity in the face of Georgia's flaunting of federal authority stands in sharp contrast to his vigorous defense of federal law during South Carolina's attempt to evade the tariff during the Nullification Crisis of 1832. The principle of federal supremacy reigned even if its application was left to the discretion of the presidential administration.

The dispossession of the Native Americans relied on an appeal to biblical scripture for its ultimate justification. Advocates of removal argued that the fertile lands of the Southeast were reserved for the "cultivators of the earth." Senator Thomas Hart Benton of Missouri asserted the rights of Americans to the lands because they "used it according to the intentions of the Creator." To those who ridiculed the idea of basing the dispossession of Indian peoples on biblical principle, John Quincy Adams replied that it was "the best argument we had."

Arguments justifying removal on the grounds that the earth was reserved for tillers of the soil were rendered absurd by the fact that most of the Indians who were uprooted were themselves farmers. Many Americans were shocked and horrified at the forced relocation westward, seemingly in violation of every principle of law and justice. President Andrew Jackson answered these critics in his "removal speech" of 1830: "What good man would prefer a country covered with forests and ranged by a few thousand savages to our extensive Republic? . . . And is it supposed that a wandering savage has a stronger attachment to his home than the settled civilized Christian?"

THE CONQUEST OF SPACE

Even as late as 1800, few Americans conceived of the possibility of transcontinental dominion. The distances seemed too great, the obstacles to maintaining political and economic unity too immense, to entertain such an idea. Jefferson, while he hoped to expel the European colonial influence throughout the entire continent, envisioned the United States bordered on the west by one or more sister republics. Securing the domain east of the Rockies seemed challenging enough. Senator Thomas Hart Benton, one of the most ardent expansionists, declared in 1825 that the Rocky Mountains formed the natural western boundary of the country: "Along the back of this ridge the Western limit of the republic should be drawn, and the statue of the fabled god Terminus should be raised upon its highest peak, never to be thrown down."

Rapidly evolving transportation and communication technologies, combined with an ebullient American nationalism, soon altered the sense of what was possible. By 1820 steamboats had turned the nation's unparalleled system of rivers into an invaluable interstate transportation network navigable in all directions. An extensive system of canals, whose construction costs often were subsidized by state and local governments, complemented this system.

The "transportation revolution" accelerated in the 1820s

with the development of the railroad. Railroads offered the revolutionary possibility that bulk goods might be shipped long distances to market at low cost, thus enhancing the profit potential of interior agricultural regions. By the early 1840s the entrepreneur Asa Whitney was urging the construction of a transcontinental railroad. Whitney envisioned it as a direct link from Europe to the East Asia trade. He mused in a letter to Secretary of the Treasury Robert J. Walker that such a link "would place us in a position to defy and, if we please, dictate to all the world."

The unprecedented immensity of a transcontinental railroad construction project, combined with the Democratic party's ideological reluctance to involve the federal government in such a scheme, placed Whitney's grandiose vision on hold. Nonetheless by 1850 the nation was crisscrossed by more than 9,000 miles of track. By 1860 that number had risen to 30,600 miles—more than in all of continental Europe combined. Senator Stephen Douglas of Illinois defended the rapid and unprecedented growth of the American empire by appealing to the wonders of technology: "The application of steam power to transportation and travel has brought the remotest limits of the confederacy, now comprising twenty-six states—much nearer to the centre than when there were but thirteen.... The facilities and rapidity of our communication are increasing in a much greater ratio than our territory or population." Amazingly the nation's technological development seemed to be able to keep pace with its messianic expansionist ambitions.

Colonel J. J. Abert, head of the army Corps of Topographical Engineers, emphasized the importance of a transcontinental railroad to the maintenance of the Union in a letter to a State Department official in 1849, after the acquistion of California: "The consequences of such a road are immense. They probably involve the integrity of the Union. Unless some easy, cheap, and rapid means of communicating with these distant provinces be accomplished, there is danger, great danger, that they will not constitute parts of our Union. Then what will become of our great moral power, our great commerce, our infinite resources?"

The development of the telegraph in the 1840s further solidified the bonds of the increasingly far-flung Union. Near-instantaneous communication promised, as the newspaper publisher James Gordon Bennett put it, "to blend into one homogeneous mass . . . the whole population of the Republic." Senator Lewis Cass of Michigan rhapsodized that "As we increase in numbers and extend in space, our power of communication is still more augmented. . . . The telegraph has come with its wonderful process to bind still closer the portions of this empire, as they recede from its capital."

The new transportation and communication technologies promised to conquer the vast distances that had seemed to limit the growth of the American empire. When combined with American political institutions, they offered the possibility of open-ended expansionism. Writing in the *Democratic Review,* John L. O'Sullivan envisioned the United States encompassing all of North America because its government was "organized under that admirable federative principle which can govern equally a continent or a county." Modern technology had created "a vast skeleton framework of railroads, and an infinitely ramified nervous system of magnetic telegraphs" which could bind the empire as one. Surely God had given to the American people the tools they needed to realize their apparent destiny to spread across the continent, throughout the hemisphere, indeed, around the globe. Or so many Americans thought at the time.

4

Texas and Oregon

"If a man is disappointed in politics or in love he goes and buys land."—Harriet Martineau, 1830s

NO SOONER HAD the U.S. claim to Texas been formally conceded by final ratification of the Transcontinental Treaty with Spain than Americans began migrating to the province. In 1820 Moses Austin, lured by the promises of Spanish officials of substantial land grants along the Brazos River, led three hundred families into Texas. The new government of the Republic of Mexico proved even more generous. In an effort to boost migration into the sparsely populated region, the Mexican government offered 4,428 acres of land for about $200, payable in installments. At the time this compared to a price of $1.25 per acre, payable in cash, for land in the United States. Settlers poured across the Louisiana boundary into east Texas, assured that their Protestant religion and slave property would be respected in Catholic Mexico.

By 1830 approximately twenty thousand American immigrants lived in Texas, significantly outnumbering the local Mexican population. Fearful that Texas was being lost to the enterprising and ambitious newcomers, the Mexican govern-

ment moved to discourage immigration by prohibiting the
further introduction of slaves and threatening to abolish slavery entirely. The establishment in 1834 in Mexico City of a
dictatorship under General López de Santa Anna resulted in
new efforts to assert centralized control over the distant
northern province. When Santa Anna suspended the Mexican
constitution and sent in troops to enforce his authority over
Texas, the "Texicans" revolted.

The Texas independence movement gained critical support
from the many Americans who had entered Texas in the early
1830s with the explicit aim of making the province part of the
United States. For many of the newcomers, such as Davy
Crockett of Tennessee, Texas offered a stage upon which to
revive their own fading fortunes, a new speculative frontier
where they might get rich quick. In the United States, widespread sympathy for the Texas rebels led to an outpouring of
men, money, and supplies moving across the Louisiana border
into Texas, a clear violation of American neutrality laws
which the Jackson administration claimed it was unable to
halt.

The federal government's protestations that it could not
prevent the activities of the Texas revolutionaries in Louisiana
are not persuasive when one compares its response to a similar
situation in 1837 on the Canadian border. There a minor rebellion in Canada brought a quick and effective crackdown
against Americans who planned to cross the border and aid
the revolt, thereby heading off an angry British response. In
Texas the story was different. Mexico's weak grasp over bor-
derland regions opened the door to an armed revolt that the
U.S. government welcomed. Jackson wanted Texas as much
as anyone. His and the preceding administration had made
several offers to buy Texas, all rebuffed by the Mexicans. A
number of Jackson's friends and confidants (including Sam

Houston) were leaders of the Texas revolution, and they had long urged annexation of the province.

After suffering major defeats at the Alamo and Goliad, Texan forces under Houston's command routed Santa Anna's army at the Battle of San Jacinto in April 1836. The victory ended Mexican efforts to put down the rebellion and effectively established the independence of Texas. Texans soon appealed to Washington for formal diplomatic recognition of their independence and for annexation into the Union.

But a rising chorus of opposition stayed Jackson's hand. In the first place, the Mexican government indicated it might respond to the annexation of Texas by declaring war on the United States, and Jackson did not wish to risk that possibility. War with Mexico might split the Democratic party into pro- and antislavery factions that would surely endanger the election of Martin Van Buren as Jackson's successor and might even split the Union. Jackson rebuffed the Texans' request for annexation and hesitated even to extend diplomatic recognition to the Lone Star Republic until his final day in office. Van Buren, too, as president did not push for annexation.

Even the possibility that Texas might be annexed provoked great concern. Opponents of annexation charged that Jackson was aligned with "slave holders, smugglers, Indian killers, foul-mouthed tobacco spitting men" who aimed "to carry spread-eagle supremacy from the Atlantic to the Pacific" in a backdoor attempt to bring new slave states into the Union. For the first time divisiveness over the question of slavery had hindered territorial expansion. Earlier controversies, such as the opposition of New England Federalists to the Louisiana Purchase, had been overcome either by the working of time or by compromise.

The most serious of these previous crises had occurred in 1819–1820 over the admission of Missouri as a state. That crisis had shaken the foundations of the Union—prompting Jefferson to liken it to a "firebell in the night"—until it was resolved by a compromise in which the admission of Maine as a free state balanced the admission of Missouri as a slave state. The deal's makers hoped it would "settle" the slavery question by drawing a line across the Louisiana territory at latitude 36 degrees, 30 minutes, south of which would be reserved for future slave states. The annexation of Texas, which had been excluded from the Louisiana territory by Monroe and Adams, threatened to shatter that compromise by adding an immense new territory to the dominion of slavery. Monroe had recognized the threat to the Union posed by the annexation, which is why he was willing to concede the province to Spain in the negotiations leading to the Transcontinental Treaty.

Leading the opposition to Texas annexation were the abolitionists, a numerically tiny, largely female community of conscience. Its leaders included William Lloyd Garrison, Lydia M. Child, Wendell Phillips, and Frederick Douglass. The mainstream of American society considered the abolitionists to be a lunatic fringe whose notions of equality did not stop with the freedom of slaves but extended even to equality within marriage.

The unconventional lives of many of the abolitionists invited attack by their critics. Richard Henry Dana, author of *Two Years Before the Mast,* an adventurous tale of an American in Spanish California, came away from one abolitionist meeting convinced that the movement was characterized by "radicalism, socialism, and infidelity." What did define the abolitionist movement was a deep and abiding faith that slavery was a sin in the eyes of God and must be ended everywhere, but above all in the presumed "land of the free." This spiritual zeal drove the movement in the face of ridicule, ostracism, and violence.

One of the most vocal critics of Texas annexation was the abolitionist Lydia Maria Child of Massachusetts. The youngest of six children, Child earned fame before she reached the age of thirty as a novelist and author of *The Mother's Book* (1831), which urged young women to cultivate their intellects and avoid dependence on men. After a meeting in the early 1830s with the charismatic William Lloyd Garrison, Child became a fervent and long-term advocate for abolition. In July 1833 she published *An Appeal in Favor of That Class of Americans Called Africans,* which called for immediate emancipation and made the first systematic statement of the "slave power" thesis. The controversial positions articulated in the *Appeal*—such as Child's demand for racial equality and her attack on white racism—offended mainstream tastes and cost Child her commercial popularity. But this did not still her voice. She publicly attacked "the insane rage for annexation in this country" and the desire to acquire "the territory of our neighbors by fraud or force."

Child led the grassroots opposition to the annexation of Texas by gathering signatures on antiannexationist petitions, lobbying members of Congress, and speaking out publicly. Her arguments influenced a great many prominent male abolitionists, including William Ellery Channing, Wendell Phillips, and Charles Sumner, who affectionately referred to Child as "his teacher." Privately Child placed little faith in the nation's capacity to reform itself: "I think God will overrule events to bring about a change, long before the moral sense of this nation demands it as a matter of justice and humanity."

One of Child's disciples, Unitarian minister William Ellery Channing, characterized the Texas situation in harsh terms in a letter to Henry Clay in 1837: "The Texan revolt, if regarded in its causes and in its means of success, is criminal; and we ought in no way to become partakers of its guilt. . . ." Chan-

ning decried the spirit of aggrandizement that anxiously anticipated another huge land grab. "We are a restless people,
prone to encroachment, impatient of the ordinary laws of
progress, less anxious to consolidate and perfect than to extend
our institutions, more ambitious of spreading ourselves over a
wide space than of diffusing beauty and fruitfulness over a
narrower field. We boast of our rapid growth, forgetting that,
throughout nature, noble growths are slow. . . ."

In the same letter Channing warned of dire consequences
for the country: "To annex Texas is to declare perpetual war
with Mexico. . . . The measure will extend and perpetuate
slavery. . . . Slavery will be branded on our front as the great
Idea, the prominent feature of the country. We shall renounce
our high calling as a people, and accomplish the lowest destiny
to which a nation can be bound."

The agitation of the abolitionist fringe began to encourage
mainstream politicians to speak out on the slave question.
Former secretary of state and former president John Quincy
Adams had long privately opposed the acquisition of slave
territories and had come to regret his role in acquiring slave-
holding Florida. Now in his "second career" as a Massachusetts member of the House of Representatives, Adams
assumed the lead in opposing the expansion of slavery. Influenced by abolitionist Benjamin Lundy and his well-known
pamphlet *The Genius of Universal Emancipation,* Adams articulated a belief in the existence of a "slavocracy" which aimed
to pressure the U.S. government for annexation, even at the
cost of a war with Mexico. Adams warned of the consequences if this evil clique should successfully bring Texas into
the Union: "In the face of this House and in the face of
Heaven, I avow it as my solemn belief that the annexation of
an independent sovereign power would be *ipso facto* a dissolution of this Union. . . . The question is whether a foreign na-

tion . . . a nation damned by the reinstitution of that detested system of slavery . . . should be admitted into union with a nation of freemen." Adams and others feared that incorporation of Texas into the Union as a slave state would be but a prelude to the acquisition of a slave-holding Cuba as well.

The political influence of the "slave power" was most dramatically revealed in 1836 by Congress's imposition of the infamous "Gag Rule." The burgeoning abolitionist movement had swamped Congress with a rising tide of petitions (more than 200,000 in the years 1837–1838) demanding the end of slavery. Representative of these missives was a petition from the women of Plymouth, Massachusetts: "Thoroughly aware of the sinfulness of slavery, and the consequent impolicy and the disastrous tendency of its extension in our country, we do most respectfully remonstrate, with all our souls against the annexation of Texas to the United States."

The exercise of this most basic right angered and embarrassed Southern slaveholding interests and their Northern allies in Congress. Particularly irksome was the fact that so many of the petitioners were female or black. Congressmen Benjamin Chew Howard of Maryland, who chaired the House Committee on Foreign Affairs, felt a special need to speak out on this point: "I think that these females could have sufficient field for the exercise of their influence in the discharge of their duties to their fathers, their husbands, or their children, cheering the domestic circle and shedding over it the mild radiance of social virtues, instead of rushing into the fierce struggles of political life. I feel sorry at this departure from their proper sphere. . . ."

In response to this most unwanted flood of petitions, Congress passed a series of restrictions between 1836 and 1840 that effectively ended all congressional debate on slavery. No abolitionist petition would be received, no criticism of slavery uttered, no speculation on the role of the federal government in regulating or abolishing slavery would be tolerated within its chambers. In effect, a congressional majority of Southerners and their Northern allies had banned debate on the nation's most divisive issue. The ban effectively denied women and blacks the one way their voices could be heard in the councils of government. At the same time the emancipation of slaves had now been linked to freedom of speech for white men, for they too were prohibited from speaking to Congress on the matter. Texas remained outside the Union, yet the reason for its exclusion could not be debated by Congress.

The implications of the Gag Rule were not lost on John Quincy Adams. He wrote to a group of Quincy abolitionists: "The suspension of the right to petition, the suppression of the freedom of debate, the thirst for the annexation of Texas, the war whoop of two successive Presidents of the United States against Mexico, are all but varied symptoms of a deadly disease seated in the marrow of our bones, and that deadly disease is slavery. The Union will fall before it, or it will fall before the Union."

OREGON FEVER

As the Texas question simmered in the late 1830s and early 1840s, American expansionists increasingly directed their attention toward the Oregon territory. A formal U.S. claim to the region dated from the Convention of 1818 with Great Britain, which enacted a policy of "free and open occupation" for citizens of both nations for a period of ten years. The Transcontinental Treaty of 1819 reinforced that claim by establishing a boundary to the Pacific Ocean along the 42nd parallel. At that time the region's chief appeal was as a source of furs for export to China.

The dream of a commercial empire centered in Astoria, Oregon, failed to materialize, though not for lack of interest. During the 1820s Congressman John Floyd of Virginia pushed for American military occupation of the Columbia River for the purpose of encouraging trade with China. Treacherous shoals, however, prevented Astoria from becoming a major port, and overhunting decimated the population of sea otters, formerly a key fur export to Canton. The Adams administration did renew the "free and open occupation" agreement for an indefinite period when it expired in 1827.

By the late 1830s interest began to build in faraway Oregon as a site for agricultural settlement. Protestant missionaries, hearing tales of Flathead Indians who hungered for Christian redemption, journeyed west to spread the gospel and win converts among local Indians. In 1834 the missionary Jason Lee established a mission in the Willamette Valley; by 1836 he was joined by Marcus and Narcissa Whitman, who endeavored to save native souls at an outpost near present-day Walla Walla. Although epidemic disease and native skepticism limited the success of the missionaries in converting Indians, the evangelists' glowing letters telling of Oregon's fertile valleys and mild climate aroused the interest of those seeking a fresh start in a new land. Soon American settlers overwhelmed both the Indians and the employees of the Hudson Bay Company. Migration was also encouraged by Washington Irving's novel *Astoria* (1836), which heralded Oregon's "mildness and equability of climate."

More than a few of Oregon's first American pioneers were fleeing the financial embarrassments of the Panic of 1837 and its subsequent depression, the worst economic downturn in the nation's history to that time. In this regard Oregon functioned only as the newest largely unexploited economic frontier for the nation's surplus population—as Texas had before.

BRITISH
NORTH
AMERICA

Ft. Simpson

54° 40' N

Natural Boundary of Oregon

Pacific
Ocean

Ft. Alexandria

DISPUTED
AREA

Fraser River

Line of 1846

Vancouver
Island

Line of 1818

Ft. Victoria

Ft. Colville

Missouri River

*Columbia
River*

○ Spokane

Ft. Vancouver

Portland ○

○ Lewiston
Ft. Walla Walla

UNITED
STATES

Ft. Boise

Oregon Trail

Ft. Hall

Ft. Bridger

SETTLEMENT OF THE OREGON BOUNDARY, 1846

By the early 1840s the "Oregon Trail" had become a deeply rutted highway for thousands in search of the American Dream. Lord Castlereagh's observation to an American diplomat of some years before—"You will conquer Oregon in your bedchambers"—appeared to be coming true.

As the numbers of Americans in Oregon grew, so did the stridency of the American claim to the vaguely defined territory. As with Louisiana, the open-ended boundaries of Oregon dazzled the American imagination. Captain Gray's voyage to the Columbia River region in the 1780s was supplemented by Lewis and Clark's foray overland, yet those thrusts did little to establish a clearly demarcated claim. By the 1830s the region's boundaries west of the Rocky Mountains extended from the 42nd parallel (the present-day boundary with California) northward, at least to the Columbia River country, probably to the Puget Sound area, and possibly, in the wildest dreams of expansionists, as far north as 54 degrees, 40 minutes north latitude. Blocking this grandiose pretension was Great Britain, who, with the Indians of the region, had a stronger claim to ownership and no inclination to yield.

Faced with this obstruction and always desirous of providing their imperial dominion with at least the appearance of moral and ethical righteousness, Americans evolved arguments justifying their claim. They did so by replacing the doctrines of international law (whose precedents in this case favored the British) with a code of natural law that privileged the claims of those nations "contiguous" to a given territory. As early as 1823 John Quincy Adams had made this argument in a letter to Minister Richard Rush in London, foreshadowing the "noncolonization clause" of the Monroe Doctrine: "It is not imaginable that any European nation should entertain the project of settling a colony on the Northwest Coast of America. That the United States should form establishments there ... is not only to be expected, but is pointed out by the finger of nature. . . ." As the 1840s unfolded, the trickle of settlers into Oregon was characterized by some members of Congress as "the never-ceasing advance of a rising tide of the sea," and possession of Oregon took on the appearance of a providential right.

"DANGER FROM ABROAD"

As interest in Oregon mounted, proponents of Texas annexation redoubled their efforts. In 1842 rumors of a Mexican plot to invade Texas provoked calls for American intervention. Not long after that scare proved a false alarm, widespread fear arose among slavery expansionists that Great Britain planned to intrude itself in some way in the affairs of the Texas Republic.

These fears were not entirely groundless. London had abolished slavery within the empire in 1834. British abolitionists, as part of a campaign to abolish slavery elsewhere, now pushed their government for an "emancipationist loan" to the Texans as a means of ending slavery and bringing the Texas Republic into the orbit of Great Britain. Developing close ties with an independent Texas offered a number of distinct advantages to the British. Chief among these was the possibility that an independent Texas within the British sphere of influence would block American expansion to the Southwest. British policy had long wished to contain the growth of the United States even as it cultivated commercial ties with the Americans. In addition, the Lone Star Republic could serve as an alternative source of cotton for British textile mills as well as provide a growing market for British manufactured exports. The Texans, for their part, welcomed Britain's interest and embraced a plan suggested by Lord Aberdeen: England

and France would secure recognition of Texas by Mexico and guarantee the integrity of the borders of both states.

Southerners and proslavery activists viewed the British moves in Texas with alarm. Bad enough that the British presumed to interpose themselves in the path of the American imperial juggernaut. Proslavery elements opposed abolition anywhere as a threat to the continuation of the "peculiar institution" everywhere. The cry arose in the press and Congress that a "danger from abroad" threatened to stymie fulfillment of America's destiny. By raising the specter of European intervention, proannexationist elements hoped to rebuild national unity by diverting attention from the internal debate over slavery and focusing instead on an external enemy.

Their efforts to do so were helped immensely by the accession of John Tyler to the presidency in April 1841 as a result of the death of Whig president William Henry Harrison from an illness contracted at his inauguration. Tyler, a Virginian, slaveholder, and longtime proponent of acquiring Texas, had been a Democrat until he changed parties shortly before the 1840 election. Mockingly known as "His Accidency" for the way in which he became president, Tyler quickly fell out of favor with leaders of the Whig party. To their consternation, he made negotiation of an annexation treaty his priority.

Tyler was assisted in his efforts by a cadre of boosters, speculators, and journalists. One of the most zealous and energetic of these was Duff Green of Maryland. Entrepreneur, speculator, journalist, and arch-propagandist for Manifest Destiny, Green journeyed to London in 1841 ostensibly to discuss prospects for a trade reciprocity treaty but actually to confirm British intentions in Texas. Seeing what he wanted to see and finding what he wanted to find, in 1842 Green returned to the United States warning of British plans to contain American power by abolishing slavery in Texas. Britain, he wrote to

Tyler, wished to ban slavery in order to strengthen its competitive position in the world economy. Green charged that
Britain's "war upon slavery is a war on our commerce and
manufactures—through our domestic institutions." The consequences of British policy had already proved catastrophic. In
a letter to Secretary of State John C. Calhoun, Green observed
that "The effect of the abolition of slavery in the British West
India colonies has been to ruin the planter, to hand over his
property to the emancipated slave and convert those islands
into black colonies of England."

   While Green's arguments exercised the fears of Southerners over Texas, Senator Robert J. Walker of Mississippi, at the
request of his personal friend President Tyler, took on the
more challenging task of explaining to Northerners why annexation was in their interest. In early 1844 he did so in a public statement of position entitled "Letter of Mr. Walker . . .
Relative to the Annexation of Texas." Walker appealed directly to the fears of Northern whites by suggesting that if
abolitionists were successful in stopping the annexation of
Texas, they would eventually be able to end slavery in the
United States. In this way Walker linked the question of slavery with the question of race and the uncertain future emancipation would bring. He raised the specter of three million
freed slaves migrating north, inundating the "free states" with
a population "wretched in condition and debased in morals."
Walker cynically used the census of 1840 (the first to gather
statistics on mental and physical ailments in the population) to
claim that Northern free blacks were far more likely to be
deaf, dumb, insane, infirm, or criminal than was the case of
blacks in slavery. The message was clear—slavery was essential to both the well-being of blacks and to the well-being of
white America.

   Although his census statistics were later shown to be—to

say the least—a misinterpretation of the data (in Worcester, Massachusetts, for example, 133 of 151 blacks were listed as insane), Walker's message was widely reprinted in the nation's press and made an undeniable impression on the public mind. Walker held out only one hope for the United States to avoid the catastrophe he envisioned: annex Texas immediately. Only then would the institution of slavery be safe, and only then would slaveowners in the other states of the South have a place to sell their own slaves when soil exhaustion made their enterprises unprofitable. With Texas as a "safety valve," the black population would be "diffused" into the Southwest and from there migrate into Mexico and Central America. There blacks could attain the equality unavailable to them in the United States. Thus America would have a solution to its race problem: the removal of blacks from the country. Walker characterized annexation as "essential to the security of the South, the defence of the West, and highly conducive to the welfare and perpetuity of the Union." Annexationists had cast territorial expansion not just as possible or desirable but as necessary to the survival of the Union.

Amidst this effort to scare the public into supporting annexation, Secretary of State Calhoun, one of slavery's most zealous defenders, took charge of negotiations with Texas. First, however, he issued a stern warning to Britain about the consequences of encouraging abolition in Texas. In a letter to the British minister to the United States, Richard Pakenham, in April 1844, later released to the press, Calhoun made clear what the stakes of the situation were. Warning the British to confine their abolitionist tendencies to their own possessions, Calhoun linked slavery to national survival: ". . . It may be asserted that what is called slavery, is in reality, a political institution essential to the peace, safety, and prosperity of those States of the Union in which it exists." He pledged to wield

the power of the federal government in defense of that "essential" American political institution.

By early 1844 the Texas question dominated national politics. Andrew Jackson, a formidable influence even in retirement, made his feelings known in a letter to W. B. Lewis in
April 1844. Texas, Jackson wrote, must be acquired "peaceably if we can, forcibly if we must." Tyler reemphasized the
importance of Texas in a message to Congress on April 22,
1844: "The country itself thus obtained is of incalculable value
in an agricultural and commercial point of view. To the soil of
inexhaustible fertility it unites a genial and healthy climate,
and is destined at a day not distant to make a large contribu-
tion to the commerce of the world. . . . The question is one
purely American."

The government of Mexico disagreed. Still unreconciled to
the loss of Texas, the Mexicans pledged to retaliate if it was annexed by the United States. Polk, unlike Jackson, seems not to
have been fazed by this prospect.

Calhoun did succeed in negotiating an annexation treaty
with the Texans, but its chances for ratification by a two-
thirds majority of the Senate were dashed by the publication
of his letter to Pakenham and by Calhoun's public boast that
annexation was "the most effectual, if not the only means
of guarding against the threatened danger" of abolition.
Fears that Britain aimed to bottle up American westward
expansion were now overwhelmed by fears that a conspiracy
of slaveholders aimed to bring Texas into the Union primarily
to defend slavery. Consequently in June 1844 Northern
and Western expansionists joined with antislavery senators
to defeat the annexation treaty 35 to 16—a two-thirds
majority *against* annexation. Nearly a decade after winning
its independence from Mexico, Texas remained outside the
Union.

THE ELECTION OF 1844

By 1844 the nation was split over the question of Texas. The matter had become a lightning rod in the division over slavery, both internally and internationally. Yet the slavery question was but one of a number of issues regarding the future of the empire that threatened to tear the nation apart. At the heart of the question was a divergence in philosophy over alternate courses of national development.

Members of the Whig party, from whatever region, pushed for greater centralized direction and control over the country. Whigs supported a national bank (assailed by the Jacksonians as a "monster"), an extensive system of federally financed internal improvements, and a protective tariff for industry. In foreign affairs Whigs pushed vigorously for commercial expansion but often favored restraint in expanding the nation's territorial holdings.

Democrats, the self-conscious party of the people formed in the wake of the Jacksonian revolution, were just as inclined to oppose an activist role for the federal government. They fought the Second Bank of the United States as a dangerous concentration of economic power, resisted federally financed internal improvements as unconstitutional (although they often backed state-supported improvements), and sought to lower or eliminate the tariff.

Paradoxically the Democrats' advocacy of limited government did not preclude the use of the American army to remove Indians from the Southeast, or the use of the navy to support American commercial expansion overseas. The most significant difference between the two parties was the Democrats' push for expansion in order to provide an ever-expanding frontier for migration-minded Americans. In this way the Democrats hoped permanently to export the nation's social problems into new frontiers of opportunity. In a sense the Jacksonians merely took Jefferson's logic regarding the acquisition of Louisiana and extended it to, potentially, the entire hemisphere. To the Whig proposal of perfecting the country through internal improvements, the Democrats replied with a program of breakneck expansion.

In 1844 champions of Manifest Destiny in Congress and in the press launched an all-out campaign to expand across the continent. Perhaps it followed from the growing sense of American "exceptionalism," perhaps it was designed to take people's minds off the stubbornly persistent economic depression. In any case, the avalanche of rhetoric and boosterism proved difficult to resist. The early belief that the American republic had a limit beyond which it could not grow was replaced by an exuberant sense that the nation could expand indefinitely. The ideology of American Manifest Destiny reached its apex in the mid-1840s. Emanating from the press, Congress, and the alehouse, Manifest Destiny was a yeasty brew of self-interest, superheated nationalism, racism, and a lachrymose idealism.

A key slogan fueling the expansionist fervor was the concept of "extending the area of freedom." The phrase first appeared in a letter from Jackson made public in 1844, and it encapsulated the boisterous optimism and egoism of the time. The concept was a variant of the familiar theme of America's mission to redeem the world. The theory was that European "absolutism," by its presumed attempts to gain control of Texas, threatened the "republicanism" of the United States. The need to extend the area of freedom was thus given special urgency by the perception that Texas—the region to which the phrase most often referred—was at risk of being "lost" to European absolutism.

In order to ease the concerns of Northerners that expansion

into Texas was little more than a conspiracy of slaveholders, Democrats trumpeted their support for simultaneously acquiring Oregon. Here again the rhetoric of Manifest Destiny proved able to sway the masses, this time through the assertion that whatever the legal and historical arguments, the United States held "the true title" to Oregon. Calhoun intimated this in an official communication to the British in which he claimed that Oregon "is destined to be peopled by us." The gist of the argument was that America's superior virtue and agricultural population, in addition to the presumed contiguous nature of Oregon to the rest of the United States, made the territory "naturally" an American possession.

Expansionist firebrands began to call for the "reoccupation" of Oregon at the earliest possible moment, a reference to the free and open occupation agreement with Great Britain first reached in 1818. They called for the United States to assert its claim as far north as 54 degrees, 40 minutes, and fight if the British did not yield entirely. The British made it clear they would resist American expansionist ambitions in the region, even at the cost of war. But Manifest Destiny had made continental dominion its formal goal. Illinois Senator Sidney Breese asserted that "our confederacy is peculiarly adapted to expansion, and any number of states can be added to it, strengthening it by their number, until its circumference shall embrace all the territory of this continent."

The twin expansionist ambitions of the Democrats were given tangible form at the party's 1844 nominating convention for president in Baltimore. Extravagant expansionist rhetoric marked the gathering. Major August Davezac of New Jersey, comrade in arms of Jackson in the War of 1812, suggested, to great applause, the limits of the expansionists' yearnings: "Land enough—land enough! Make way, I say, for the young American Buffalo—he has not yet got enough land; he wants more land as his cool shelter in summer—he wants more land for his beautiful pasture grounds. I tell you, we will give him Oregon for his summer shade, and the region of Texas, as his winter pasture.... Like all of his race, he wants salt, too. Well, he shall have the use of two oceans—the mighty Pacific and the turbulent Atlantic shall be his.... He shall not stop his career until he slakes his thirst in the frozen ocean." High-flown rhetoric, to be sure, but amidst the foot-stomping, cigar-smoking, whiskey-drinking atmosphere that pervaded Baltimore's Odd Fellows Egyptian Hall, anything seemed possible.

The Democrats emerged from their caucus with a party platform asserting that "our title to the whole of the territory of Oregon is clear and unquestionable; that no portion of the same ought to be ceded to England or any other power; and that the re-occupation of Oregon and the re-annexation of Texas at the earliest practicable period are great American measures...." An expansionist gauntlet built on dubious historical assertions had been defiantly thrown down, risking war with two nations.

Equally significant, the party's Calhoun faction enforced an 1836 decision that changed the margin needed for nomination from a simple majority to a two-thirds majority. This denied the nomination to former president and odds-on favorite Martin Van Buren, who opposed the annexation of Texas. On the forty-fourth ballot, the Democrats nominated an ardent expansionist, Jackson protégé, and relative political unknown, James Knox Polk of Tennessee.

By 1844, however, the protests of the abolitionists began to spread to broader segments of the Northern white population. While slavery had been controversial from the time of the Constitutional Convention, in the summer of 1844 a growing number of white Northerners became acutely aware (as John

Quincy Adams had been for some years) that the institution affected all Americans, white and black. Known as antislavery advocates to distinguish themselves from abolitionists, these opponents of slavery cared little if any for the plight of blacks, but they cared immensely about their future economic prospects in a slave-labor economy in which those without the capital to buy slaves faced little hope of becoming well-to-do. While antislavery advocates accepted the argument that the immediate abolition of slavery was impractical and potentially chaotic, they feared the peculiar institution's spread into the new states to be carved out of the imperial domain.

Slavery, an inflammatory question since the Constitutional Convention of 1787, could not be excluded from the national debate. In spite of the Gag Rule in Congress, the censorship of the mails, the destruction of abolitionist newspapers, and the harassment and murder of abolitionists, the argument over the nature of American freedom—and thus over the nature of the American nation and American empire—could not be stifled.

One sign of rising tensions was the repeal in 1844 of the congressional Gag Rule, thanks largely to the untiring efforts of John Quincy Adams. Now the voices of opposition could be heard. Joshua Giddings, representative from Ohio and a leading congressional opponent of the slave power, warned of the consequences for the nation if Texas were annexed: ". . . We shall not surrender this Union, sanctioned and sanctified by half a century of national prosperity, in order to try a new union, and that too, with slave holding Texas! Sir, every school boy must see that to form a new union with any foreign power, would be, ipso facto, a dissolution of our present Union."

Henry Clay, the Whig party's nominee for president in 1844, staked out his position early in the campaign in his

widely reprinted "Raleigh" letter. Clay unambiguously opposed expansion: "I consider the annexation of Texas, at this
time, without the assent of Mexico, as a measure compromising the national character, involving us certainly in a war with
Mexico, probably with other foreign powers, dangerous to the
integrity of the Union, inexpedient to the present financial
condition of the country, and not called for by any general ex-
pression of public opinion." Clay hoped this unambiguous
statement of his position would unify abolitionist and antislavery factions behind his candidacy.

Yet by the close of the campaign the rhetoric of Manifest
Destiny had unleashed a rising expansionist fervor that Clay,
always a cagey politician, could not ignore. Opinion in the
press and in the alehouse seemed strong for expansion. In a
tight race with Polk, Clay late in the campaign announced
that he did not oppose Texas annexation and in fact would "be
glad to see it, without dishonor, without war, with the common consent of the Union, and upon just and fair terms." In a
presidential race dominated as few have been before or since
by foreign policy issues, Clay's waffling proved fatal to his
chances for success. In the razor-close election New Yorkers
cast five thousand votes for antislavery candidate James K.
Birney, probably costing Clay the Empire State's thirty-six
electoral votes and consequently the election. James K. Polk of
Tennessee, slaveholder and unabashed expansionist, now occupied the White House.

"THE APOPLEXY OF THE CONSTITUTION"

Although Polk had won the election by a narrow majority
both in the popular vote and in the electoral college, President
Tyler interpreted the result as mandate to take Texas. He now
boldly acted to accomplish the deed before the inauguration of

his successor. Unable to gain the necessary two-thirds majority needed for the Senate to ratify an annexation treaty, Tyler resorted to annexation via a "joint resolution" of the Congress that would require only a simple majority of both houses for passage. Thus during the lame-duck session before the inauguration of Polk, Congress annexed Texas by joint resolution, 120 to 98 in the House and 27 to 25 in the Senate. After a nine-year struggle, on March 1, 1845, Tyler signed the legislation offering Texas admission into the Union. Mexico reacted to annexation "as equivalent to a declaration of war" and recalled its minister from Washington. Diplomatic relations between the two countries were soon suspended.

Abolitionists and antislavery activists were outraged by Tyler's audacity. Slavery expansionists, frustrated in their attempts to acquire Texas, had made an end run around the Constitution. Old-time Jeffersonians, such as Albert Gallatin, were shocked at the high-handedness of the move. Gallatin labeled the tactic "an undisguised usurpation of power." John Quincy Adams spoke in even graver terms. On the day the Senate approved annexation, he wrote in his diary: ". . . the heaviest calamity that ever befell myself and my country was this day consummated. . . . I regard it as the apoplexy of the Constitution."

On March 3 House opponents of annexation responded loudly and publicly to events: ". . . We hesitate not to say that annexation, effected by any act or proceeding of the federal government, or any of its departments, would be identical with dissolution . . . and we not only assert that the people of the free states 'ought not to submit to it,' but we say, with confidence, they would not submit to it." It seemed that annexing Texas might destroy rather than expand the Union.

Not surprisingly, slavery expansionists heralded the unexpected victory. Congressman Chesselden Ellis of New York argued the righteousness of the final outcome of the Texas question. It was, he said, "a territory intended for the possession and destiny of the American race—an outline drawn by the hand of the Creator himself. . . . Why wing the eagle on his bold ascent towards the sun? The sky was given for his dominion. Why strip him of his plumage, and fix him to the earth? Sir, you cannot, if you would, set bounds to the indomitable energy of our noble race. . . . To arrest our peaceful and onward march would be treason to the cause of human liberty."

President Polk was delighted by Tyler's ploy. Now he would not have to waste political capital in a tough fight to gain a two-thirds majority for annexation in the Senate. In his inaugural address he defiantly challenged both the anti-expansionists and the Mexicans. "I regard the question of annexation as belonging exclusively to the United States and Texas. . . . None can fail to see the danger to our safety and future peace if Texas remains an independent state or becomes an ally or dependency of some foreign nation more powerful than herself. . . ." With Texas in hand, Polk could concentrate his energies on Oregon and, more important as far as he was concerned, California.

Since the early 1830s American interest in California had risen steadily. Andrew Jackson, described by John Quincy Adams as having a "passion" for San Francisco Bay, tried unsuccessfully in 1835 to buy that capacious harbor and all of California north of the 38th parallel. Amidst the Texas controversy, Mexico rebuffed Jackson's offer. In 1842 Tyler too had tried and failed to buy California, if only to keep it out of the hands of the British, who, it was thought, were trying to intrude themselves into the area. Fears that Britain planned to seize California in the event of an American-Mexican clash spurred Thomas Ap Catesby Jones to sail a naval squadron into Monterey in 1842 and claim California for the United States. When the rumor of war proved false, Jones ignominiously hauled down the American flag, but the nation's interest in the province remained. Polk eyed California primarily for its three magnificent harbors—San Francisco, Monterey, and San Diego—which offered a gateway to the commerce of the Pacific.

While Polk plotted, a rising chorus of voices sang of limitless expansion. Preparing for a massive land grab, Manifest Destiny's proponents proclaimed their country's special virtue. John L. O'Sullivan trumpeted that "No instance of aggrandizement or lust for territory has stained our annals. No nation has been despoiled by us, no people overrun." James Gordon Bennett, owner of the *New York Herald* and archexpansionist, explained that the United States was "the only power which has never sought and never seeks to acquire a foot of territory by force of arms." Along the same lines, the *United States Journal* cited those self-evident reasons why expansion was not only desirable but foreordained: ". . . We the American people, are the most independent, intelligent, moral and happy people on the face of the earth."

As the Oregon question continued to hang fire, expansionists cast about for a formula to justify beyond refutation the American claim. O'Sullivan dispensed with legalities in his landmark article "The True Title," which appeared in the *New York Morning News* of December 27, 1845. Arguing for American control of Oregon, O'Sullivan boldly mused, ". . . Were the respective cases and arguments of the two parties, as to all these points of history and law, reversed . . . our claim to Oregon would still be best and strongest. And that claim is by our right of our manifest destiny to overspread and to possess the whole of the continent which Providence has given us for the development of the great experiment of liberty and feder-

ated self-government entrusted to us." Representative Robert
Winthrop heralded "the right of our manifest destiny to
spread over this whole continent."

With this rhetoric at his back, Polk confidently moved to
increase the pressure on Great Britain and Mexico. In July he
ordered General Zachary Taylor and four thousand troops to
take a position on the west bank of the Nueces River—disputed territory claimed by Mexico—and to guard the mouth
of that river from invasion. Polk also deployed a U.S. navy
squadron to the Gulf of Mexico to support Taylor in the event
of hostilities. Next he sent emissary John Slidell to Mexico
City to push for a settlement of all issues, including extending
the Texas boundary to the Rio Grande and purchasing all or
part of New Mexico and California. In case the Slidell mission
should fail, Polk appointed Thomas D. Larkin as his confidential special agent to travel to California and foment an independence movement among the small American population
there—a first step toward uniting "their destiny with ours."

Polk moved first to confront Britain over Oregon and re-
assure the tiny American settlements in the region that the
federal government was ready to support their claims. Instructions dated December 5, 1846, ordered Commodore John
D. Sloat, commanding the Pacific Squadron then stationed off
Mexico's western coast, to captain a naval vessel to the Columbia River and thence to the Strait of San Juan de Fuca. Sloat
was to distribute five hundred copies of the president's message to Congress announcing his bold stand for Oregon to settlers in the Willamette Valley. The commodore was also
empowered to trade any rifles or small arms in his possession
for agricultural produce, "taking all possible care that they fall
into the hands of no one who is unfriendly to the United
States. *These orders you will keep secret*" [emphasis mine].

Some members of Congress kept up the pressure on Polk to

confront the British in Oregon. Not the least of them was John Quincy Adams, whose anti-Texas stand did not diminish his enthusiasm for "All of Oregon." In January 1846 Adams asked the clerk to read to the House of Representatives the biblical injunction to "Be fruitful and multiply, and replenish the earth, and subdue it; and have dominion over the fish of the sea, and over the fowl of the air, and over every living thing that moveth upon the earth." "There, Sir!" Adams triumphantly proclaimed, "There in my judgment is the foundation not only of our title to Oregon, but the foundation of all human title to all human possessions." Manifest Destiny stood on the verge of consummation—it seemed to be both the will of the people and the will of God.

Polk, in his annual message to the new session of Congress on December 2, 1845, prepared the ground for his expansionist policy in the first public reassertion of the Monroe Doctrine since its principles were first uttered in Monroe's 1823 address. Polk proclaimed the doctrine's basic principles of American supremacy and prohibition on further European colonization in the Western Hemisphere: "The people of the United States can not . . . view with indifference attempts of European powers to interfere with the independent action of the nations on this continent. . . ." He then quoted directly from Monroe's message: "The American continents, by the free and independent condition which they have assumed and maintained, are henceforth not to be considered as subjects for future colonization by any European powers." Polk had reasserted the doctrine of U.S. hemispheric superiority. But how would he apply it?

5

The Conquest of Mexico

"Our nation's bigger 'n theirn, an' so its rights air bigger."
—Private First Class Birdofredom Sawin

THE SPIRIT OF Manifest Destiny swept over the land in the wake of the annexation of Texas. Surely God's divine will had taken one step closer to realization with the incorporation of a massive new state into the Union. Continued uncertainty about the Mexican government's reaction to annexation, and Britain's response to the Oregon dispute, prompted calls for a direct confrontation with those who would resist America's expansionist destiny. An editorial in the *New York Globe* (February 18, 1846) suggested that it was the "duty of our government to *seek* rather than *evade* a war with" Great Britain. Representative Andrew Kennedy of Indiana decried signs of submissiveness to the British "lion" in Oregon. He counseled the United States to stand tall when confronting the "King of beasts": "We will not go out of our way to seek a conflict with him; but if he crosses our path, and refuses to move at a peaceful command, he will run his nose in the talons of the American eagle, and his blood will spout as from a harpooned whale."

Other voices in the press had been for some time equally if not more vehement for war. "LET US GO TO WAR" shouted the headline of the *New York Journal of Commerce* on May 21, 1845. "The world has become stale and insipid, the ships ought to be all captured, and the cities battered down, and the world burned up, so that we can start again. There would be fun in that." A Cincinnati newspaper welcomed war as a necessary part of human progress: "An occasional conflict with barbarians must be expected. . . . The loss of a few thousand of them would not be so deplorable. The Mexicans will be led by this war to think of their weakness and inferiority." Andrew Johnson of Tennessee argued that God's wrath was being unleashed against "perfidious and half-civilized Mexico" and that "the Anglo-Saxon race has been selected as the rod of her retribution."

Those who called for the fulfillment of Manifest Destiny were given a mighty assist by the proliferation of the "penny press" in the mid-1840s. The railroad, the telegraph, and even the use of the carrier pigeon all contributed to reducing the time it took to transmit the news of the day, and the invention of the high-speed press reduced printing costs and fostered the creation of a mass media with an unprecedented capacity to influence public opinion. Newspaper barons such as James Gordon Bennett of the *New York Herald* and Moses Y. Beach of the *New York Sun* titillated their readers with sensationalistic accounts of the events of the day. None proved more appealing than those dealing with Manifest Destiny, whose themes of America's special virtue, redemptionist mission, and godly ordained destiny were guaranteed to make most people feel united and good and thus sell papers.

The role of Bennett is especially noteworthy. A precursor to later media powers such as William Randolph Hearst, Bennett cloaked an expansionist political agenda which he pushed vigorously in his paper. An unrelenting critic of the abolitionists—he once said that "sympathy for the black man is but a pretence for plundering and oppressing the white"—Bennett heralded the approaching conflict with Mexico as a test of American Anglo-Saxonism. He contrasted the implicit special virtue of the United States—"the only power which has never sought and never seeks to acquire a foot of territory by force of arms"—with "the imbecility and degradation of the Mexican people," the result, he claimed, of "the amalgamation of races." The Mexicans, Bennett predicted, were "as sure to melt away at the approach of Anglo-Saxon energy and enterprise as snow before a southern sun." The Mexican people, "before a century rolls over us, will become extinct."

Bennett was not alone in his harsh characterization of Mexican civilization. Representative Orlando Ficklin of Illinois agitated for war on the grounds that "a corrupt priesthood, with an affiliated moneyed aristocracy," had "waged unceasing war upon the liberties of the people of Mexico." Ficklin described the Mexican race as "barbarous and cruel," a "sordid and treacherous people" who were "destitute of noble impulses." He asserted that "rapine, plunder, and the spoils of conquest" were "the only sentiment that animates the bosom of her people." Senator Thomas Hart Benton suggested that "the white race will take the ascendant, elevating what is susceptible to improvement—wearing out what is not." Caleb Cushing echoed these sentiments in the June 1846 issue of the *Democratic Review*: "Race is the key to much that seems obscure in the history of nations. . . . Throughout the world, the spectacle is everywhere the same, of the whiter race ruling the less white, through all gradations of color." Senator James Buchanan dismissed the possibility that the United States might be defeated in the impending conflict: "The Anglo-

Saxon blood could never be subdued by anything that claimed Mexican origin."

As war loomed, the theme of the nation's spotless virtue was often reasserted. "No instance of aggrandizement or lust for territory has stained our annals," John L. O'Sullivan assured readers of the *New York Sun*. "No nation has ever been despoiled by us, no country laid desolate, no people overrun." Thomas Ritchie, the grand old man of what was, in general, a younger generation of voices for Manifest Destiny, gave his assessment in his *Washington Daily Union*: "Our government is not extended by the sword. . . . By its own merits it extends itself."

POLK CHOOSES WAR

With a presumed electoral mandate behind him and an increasingly bellicose and vociferous public opinion providing him with cover, President Polk began to force matters with both Great Britain and Mexico. Although the battle cry of "54-40 or fight!" had proved good politics, Polk did not plan to push for that extreme and ultimately unsustainable boundary with Canada. He was, however, determined to acquire Oregon as far north as the 49th parallel. In April 1846 Congress, at Polk's urging, terminated the "joint occupancy" agreement that had maintained the peace in Oregon since 1818. Polk told one congressman that "the only way to treat John Bull [a popular nickname for the British] was to look him straight in the eye." Confrontation, even war, seemed to be in the offing.

Yet British Foreign Secretary Lord Aberdeen under no circumstances intended to allow relations with his country's most important economic partner to be disrupted once more, particularly over a claim to a distant region of diminishing economic importance. The Polk-sponsored Walker Tariff of 1846, which reduced duties on imported manufactured goods, was far more valuable to the British economy than anything Oregon had to offer. Its formerly rich harvest of furs by this time had been virtually trapped-out south of the 49th parallel. Polk's willingness to retreat from the extreme 54-40 claim provided the British the face-saving concession they needed from the Americans in order to pull out of the region south of 49 degrees. By late spring a compromise on the matter appeared imminent.

This freed Polk's hand to push his expansionist agenda in the Southwest—long his chief concern anyway. Oregon he pursued in order to mollify Northern expansionists. Acquiring California was his priority, and by April 1846 he had maneuvered matters there into a prewar state.

Polk had prepared the ground for war by dispatching John Slidell of Louisiana as his personal emissary to Mexico. Slidell's diplomatic instructions (drafted by Secretary of State James Buchanan), dated November 10, 1845, read like a manifesto preparatory to the outbreak of hostilities. "The history of no civilized nation presents . . . so many wanton attacks upon the rights of persons and property as have been endured by citizens of the United States" at the hands of Mexico. Only because Mexico was "a neighboring and sister republic" did the United States tolerate her. Slidell's main task was to acquire California, and his instructions emphasized that "The possession of the bay and harbor of San Francisco is all important to the United States." He was to warn the Mexicans against ceding California to either Britain or France, while working to acquire the province for the United States. Buchanan warned Slidell that should Great Britain gain control of San Francisco as a commercial entreat, "the consequences would be most disastrous." Slidell was empowered to negotiate for a Texas boundary at the Rio Grande and to offer as much as $25 million for all of New Mexico and California, or $20 million for California north of Monterey. Buchanan, however, made it clear that the seriousness of the situation was such that "money would be no object" to a settlement.

Instructions in hand, Slidell headed for Mexico City on a mission that was doomed from the start. Political turmoil in Mexico probably made impossible any concessions to the Americans, and Slidell's boorish, blustering manner and broken Spanish did not help matters. Officially Mexico insisted that the Texas question must be resolved before considering other issues. The government of Mexican President José Herrera refused to entertain Slidell as an envoy extraordinary and minister plenipotentiary, that is to say, invested with full diplomatic powers. The Mexicans would receive him only on an ad hoc basis—"commissioned to settle, in a peaceful and honorable manner, the questions relative to Texas." This meant nothing to Polk, who considered the Texas question already settled by the annexation by joint resolution of the previous March. Polk wanted California, and when notice came in early January 1846 of Slidell's apparent rejection, the president moved into action.

First he dispatched orders to General Zachary Taylor to advance his 4,000-man force from the west bank of the Nueces River 150 miles to the eastern bank of the Rio Grande—disputed territory claimed by both Mexico and the United States. Polk then met with Slidell upon his return to Washington in early May to ascertain directly the political situation in Mexico City. After conferring with Slidell, Polk called his cabinet together for a council of war.

On May 9, 1846, Polk expressed his view that "we had ample cause of war" and that the situation could not remain "in status quo." All in the cabinet agreed with the president

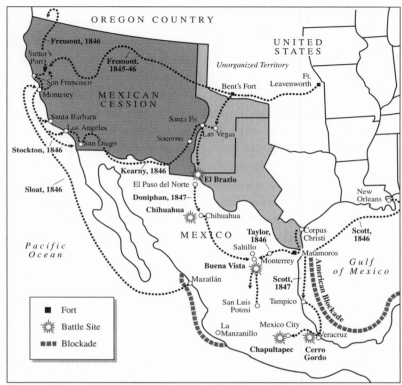

PRINCIPAL CAMPAIGNS OF THE MEXICAN WAR, 1846-1847

that circumstances warranted a declaration of war, except Secretary of the Navy George Bancroft who preferred to wait until the Mexicans committed a hostile act that would inflame public opinion. The record is clear that a decision for war had been made, with Slidell's rejection as the immediate provocation. Polk planned a formal request to Congress on Tuesday, May 12.

As fate would have it, at 6 p.m. on May 9 word arrived from the Rio Grande that Mexican forces had crossed the river and attacked Taylor's detachment, killing or wounding sixteen of his men and capturing others. Polk now had his *casus belli*. On Monday, May 11 (a day earlier than planned), he went to the Capitol to ask for a formal declaration of war.

Polk's war message reflects the self-serving logic of Manifest Destiny. In its tone and form it was reminiscent of John Quincy Adams's "great gun" of 1819. Basing his arguments on the "strong desire" of the U.S. government "to establish peace with Mexico on liberal and honorable terms," Polk recounted a long list of presumed outrages against the American government and its citizens, of which Slidell's rejection was but the last straw. Not only had the Mexican government refused honorably to discuss its differences with the United States, not only had it spurned Slidell and his olive-branch proposals, "but after a long-continued series of menaces have at last invaded our territory and shed the blood of our fellow-citizens on our own soil."

The president, in terms starkly reminiscent of those employed by Adams in his defense of Jackson's Seminole War campaign nearly thirty years earlier, cast the United States in the role of a long-aggrieved yet patient sufferer whose "cup of forbearance" had now finally been exhausted. Polk summarized: "The grievous wrongs perpetrated by Mexico upon our citizens throughout a long period of years remains unredressed, and solemn treaties pledging her public faith for this redress have been disregarded. A government either unable or unwilling to enforce the execution of such treaties fails to perform one of its plainest duties."

Polk closed his "war message" with a charge whose power to excite Congress and the public was not diminished by its dubious truthfulness: "... After repeated menaces, Mexico has passed the boundary of the United States, has invaded our territory, and shed American blood upon the American soil. . . . War exists, and notwithstanding all our efforts to avoid it, exists by the act of Mexico herself. . . ." Thus Polk cast his request for war as a defensive rather than offensive measure. But was it "American soil"? The Texas-Mexico border had long been, at best, vaguely defined, and remained in dispute at the time of Taylor's occupation. Polk's assertion was challenged by first-term congressman Abraham Lincoln of Illinois, who introduced a resolution demanding to see the alleged "spot" on American soil where blood had been shed. Lincoln characterized Polk's description of the causes of the war as the "half insane mumbling of a fever dream" of a president whose mind had been "tasked beyond its power."

In truth, however, it did not matter where the bloodshed occurred. An attack on American soldiers had taken place and, whatever the circumstances, could only be seen through the lens of American nationalism as grounds for retaliation. Such had been the case in 1819 when Jackson's Seminole War campaign had been embraced in spite of its doubtful constitutionality. This time proved no different. Congress reacted passionately to the president's remarks, voting for war on May 13 by 174 to 14 in the House of Representatives and 40 to 2 in the Senate.

The press soon echoed the intoxicating rhetoric of war. A young Walt Whitman, writing as editor of the *Brooklyn Daily Eagle*, responded enthusiastically to the news of a declaration of war: "Yes: Mexico must be thoroughly chastised!" Whitman called for "prompt and effectual hostilities. . . . Let our arms now be carried with a spirit which shall teach the world that, while we are not forward for a quarrel, America knows how to crush, as well how to expand."

Not all Americans responded so favorably to the declaration of war. The *American Whig Review,* an antiwar journal, sarcastically summarized Polk's logic: "We are the Anglo-Saxon Americans; it was our 'destiny' to possess and to rule this continent—we were *bound* to it! We were a chosen people, and this was our allotted inheritance, and we must drive out all other nations before us!" It seemed to many that an evil slaveholding, slave-expanding clique had seized power, first within the Democratic party by defeating the Van Buren nomination, then in the nation as a whole by exploiting divisions within Whig ranks. The Massachusetts legislature condemned the war as "a gigantic crime . . . unconstitutionally commenced by the President." Whig Senator Thomas Corwin of Ohio railed against what he saw as "this uneasy desire to augment our territory," which he believed "depraved the moral sense." Congressman Garret Davis of Kentucky fulminated that "It is our President who began this war." Even Senator John C. Calhoun, normally a staunch expansionist, feared that Polk was moving too fast. He termed "a sad delusion" the notion that the American way could be spread by force.

To the Halls of Montezuma

With war formally declared, the might of the Republic came down hard on Mexico. A call to arms brought 100,000 men, most of them from the South, to enlist. Large segments of the public, especially in the South and Southwest, had long itched for a fight in the name of the Alamo, in the name of the United States, or merely in the name of personal glory. Although weakened by poor communications, horrendous sanitary conditions, and at times indiscipline in the ranks, the American invasion force under General Taylor plunged into Mexico. After the skirmish in late April, Taylor counter-attacked and routed the Mexican forces at Palo Alto and Resaca de la Palma, even before Congress had formally declared war. By May 18 Taylor had captured Matamoros (on the west bank of the Rio Grande), where he awaited reinforcements. By late September the Americans had taken Monterrey. Then, in February 1847, Taylor's outnumbered force routed a Mexican army of 15,000 at Buena Vista. Northern Mexico was in American hands.

Meanwhile Polk struck in the West. By December 1846 a force under the command of Colonel Stephen Kearny had conquered Santa Fe and San Diego. That June, in the Sacramento Valley, Captain John C. Frémont, erstwhile Topographical Engineer, had organized the "Bear Flag Revolt," which temporarily established the Republic of California before requesting annexation by the United States. In July, Monterey, California, was occupied by American naval forces under the command of Commodore John D. Sloat, and by August the villages of Los Angeles and Santa Barbara were secured by Commodore Robert F. Stockton. Alta California was won for the North Americans.

All that remained was the conquest of Mexico City itself, a task that presented unexpected obstacles when Taylor, without orders, declared an armistice at Monterrey and encamped his troops. The general's rapidly increasing popularity and status as a Whig presidential hopeful made him both highly threatening to Polk and impossible to remove from command. Polk therefore turned to the commanding general of the army, Winfield Scott, to lead a force into Mexico City to compel the full capitulation desired. Scott's Whig affiliation also rubbed, but Polk had few viable alternatives to the crusty old hero of the War of 1812. On March 9, 1847, Scott's army of 14,000 men landed at Vera Cruz, the largest amphibious landing in American history to that time. Mexico City lay only about 250 miles away, via the difficult path through the high

Sierras followed by Cortés in the sixteenth century during the first conquest of Mexico.

The North American conquest of Mexico replicated the brutality of the Spanish conquistadors before them. Military commanders seemed to have little control over the actions of their men. George G. Meade, later renowned as the victor in the battle of Gettysburg, reported that American soldiers "killed five or six innocent people . . . for no other object than their own amusement. . . . They rob and steal the cattle of poor farmers, and in fact act more like a body of hostile Indians than civilized Whites. Their officers have no command or control over them. . . ." General Taylor acknowledged the unruliness of his troops: "There is scarcely a form of crime that has not been reported to me as committed by them."

Despite meeting continual guerrilla harassment and several sharp skirmishes en route, Scott's army marched onward through the mountains toward the Mexican capital, pausing only for reinforcement and resupply. By late September, American troops had entered the "Halls of Montezuma" and occupied Mexico City. The conquerors were not gracious to the defeated foe. General John A. Quitman, one of the leaders of the assault on the fortress of Chapultepec, which guarded the entrance to the capital, and then military governor of Mexico City, considered Mexico's eight million inhabitants to be "beasts of burden, with as little intellect as the asses whose burdens they share."

"ALL MEXICO!"

When the war with Mexico began, most Americans expected it to be short and decisive. Yet in spite of an uninterrupted string of victories, American invasion forces could not secure Mexico's capitulation. Guerrilla forces harassed Taylor and Scott's armies, and the costs of the war steadily rose.

In response to this unexpected turn of events, some editors and political leaders began to push for the acquisition of "all Mexico" as an indemnity. Not that many foresaw all of Mexico becoming part of the Union—far from it. The presumed shortcomings of the Mexican people, racially, religiously, and institutionally, precluded that possibility, but many nonetheless envisioned a vast American colony to the south as a source of future opportunity whose population might someday either be "uplifted" or removed. By later in 1847 President Polk had decided that the stubbornness of Mexican resistance might make the complete absorption of Mexico a necessary precondition to peace.

The "All Mexico" sentiment gained adherents in the nation's newspapers. The *Baltimore Sun,* whose publisher Arunah S. Abell was one of the more zealous editorial champions of Manifest Destiny, in October 1847 decried the deplorable conditions in Mexico and speculated, "Would it not be an act of benevolence, clothed too with an irrepressible moral sublimity, to revolutionize such a state of things, and restore the powers of government to the sovereignty of the people?" Along the same lines, on October 22, 1847, the *Boston Times* envisioned the "conquest" of Mexico as "necessarily a great blessing to the conquered. It is a task worthy of a great people, of a people who are about to regenerate the world by asserting the supremacy of humanity over the accidents of birth and fortune." On the same day the *New York Sun* echoed these sentiments, arguing that the Mexican race "is perfectly accustomed to being conquered, and the only new lesson we shall teach is that our victories will give liberty, safety, and prosperity to the vanquished, if they know enough to profit by the appearance of our stars. To *liberate* and *ennoble*—not to *enslave* and *debase*—is our mission."

The *Philadelphia Public Ledger* offered its own formulation of the situation in an editorial on December 11, 1847, urging the United States to "pursue the conquest; hold all the seaports and large cities; seize all the public property, all sources of revenue; introduce the common law and the English language as fast as possible. . . ." The editorial did not shrink from the amalgamationist implications of conquering the Mexican people: "Our Yankee fellows and the pretty señoritas will do the rest of the annexation, and Mexico will soon be Anglo-Saxonized and prepared for the confederacy."

Whatever the final outcome of the war, the American people continued to receive reassurances of the essential righteousness of their cause. On December 30, 1847, the city of Philadelphia toasted Commodore Robert F. Stockton for his victories in California. To thunderous applause, Stockton explained to a packed hall why California needed to be acquired: "I care not for the beautiful fields and healthful skies of California. I care not for her leagues of land and her mines of silver. The glory of the achievements there . . . is in the establishment of the first free press in California; in having built the first school-house in California; in having lighted up the torch of religious toleration as well as civil liberty, in California." Stockton attributed the amazing success of the outnumbered American forces in Mexico to divine intervention: "It is because the spirit of our pilgrim fathers is with us; it is because the God of armies and the Lord of hosts is with us." Stockton insisted that the purpose of the war was to redeem Mexico "from misrule and civil strife," and that the United States dare not evade its "duty before God" to accomplish that end. The assembled citizens of Philadelphia, far from the battlefield and having little in the way of direct knowledge of events in

Mexico, received Stockton's proclamations of Manifest Destiny with wild enthusiasm.

Countering the sentiment for "All Mexico" were those whose racial prejudices overruled whatever advantage the acquisition might represent. Senator Edward Hannegan of Indiana typified this view when in late February 1847 he proclaimed to Congress that "Mexico and the United States are peopled by two distinct and utterly unhomogeneous races. In no reasonable period could we amalgamate." The Mexican people, Hannegan asserted, were "utterly unfit for the blessings and the restraints of rational liberty." Congressman Samuel Gordon of New York doubted the wisdom of annexing "a perfidious and mixed race—a community of pirates and robbers," which the United States would then be obligated "to civilize, Christianize, and moralize." Indeed Andrew Donelson, envoy to Mexico, had informed Polk in March 1848 that "We can no more amalgamate with her people than with negroes."

In the press the influential *Democratic Review* cautioned in August 1847 that "The annexation of [Mexico] to the United States would be a calamity. . . ." The journal warned against adding five million "ignorant and indolent half-civilized Indians" to the nation's population. The *Augusta Daily Chronicle* candidly assessed the stakes of taking "all Mexico": "It would likely prove to be a sickening mixture, consisting of such a conglomeration of Negroes, and Rancheros, Mestizos, and Indians, with but a few Castilians." The *Cincinnati Herald* shrank from amalgamation with Mexico. How could the United States incorporate eight million Mexicans "with their idol worship, heathen superstition, and degraded mongrel races"?

The consensus position seemed to be the acquisition of any and all territory that was sparsely populated. Calhoun had declared in February 1847: "What we want is space for our growing population. . . . What we ought to avoid, is the addition of other populations, of a character not suited to our institutions." Thomas Ritchie, editor of the *Union*, echoed this view: "What we desire from Mexico is more of territory and less of population, but we have no objection to the acquisition of a few of her people along with the soil which we get."

As the nation anticipated a massive new extension of its imperial domain in early 1848, a mandate from heaven seemed to be in the process of realization. Democratic Senator Lewis Cass of Michigan affirmed: "To attempt to prevent the American people from taking possession of Mexico, if they demand it, would be as futile . . . as to undertake to stop the rushing of the cataract of Niagara." In February 1848 Sam Houston reasoned to a raucous crowd at New York's Tammany Hall that "the Mexicans are no better than Indians, and I see no reason why we should not go on in the same course now, and take their lands." Houston attributed the successes of the American army in Mexico to a "mandate from God," adding that "Americans regard this continent as their birthright." By the close of 1847 it appeared that the United States was about to swallow whole its neighbor to the south.

THE ANTIWAR MOVEMENT

From the outset, the war against Mexico had its critics. Their protests grew louder as the war dragged on and the outcome seemed to include the acquisition of a massive colony. The old warhorse John Quincy Adams served as the spiritual leader of this opposition, even if his age prevented him from assuming an active leadership role. Adams, in his final term as a congressman, refused to vote funds for military honors and urged American officers to resign their commissions rather than fight in what he deemed to be "this most unrighteous war." Yet Adams's opposition to the war did not prevent him from voting for the war appropriations bill, as did almost all members of Congress. However unjustified the war, the patriotic imperative to "support the troops" prevented members of Congress from pursuing the one course of action that could have ended the conflict.

One of the most outspoken of the war's critics was Whig Senator Thomas Corwin of Ohio. Addressing Congress in February 1847, he challenged the administration's war policy in strong language. Corwin agreed with Polk's war message that the conflict had not been sought "by the people" of the United States, and he charged that Polk "with the command of your standing army, did seek the war, and that *he* forced war upon Mexico." Ridiculing Polk's claim that Taylor's army crossed the Rio Grande to protect American citizens and property, Corwin asked, "Can it be, Mr. President, that the honest, generous, Christian people of the United States will give countenance to this egregious misrepresentation of fact— this bold falsification of history?"

Much of the Whig opposition to the war did little to ennoble the party. The Whig press tended to base its critique of Polk's policy not so much on the problem of extending slavery as on the allegedly undesirable population that would be brought into the Union if Mexico were conquered. The *American Whig Review* mused that the incorporation of an "ignorant and degraded population" would "convert the Republic which our fathers created for us into an Empire. . . ." Whigs, though they too expected and anticipated expansion throughout the hemisphere, feared that the militarism unleashed by the war would threaten liberty at home.

Congressman William Duer of New York refused to be

taken in by the expansionist cant that drove support for the war. In February 1848 he said, "If you wish plunder, this dismemberment of a sister Republic, let us stand forth like other conquerors, and plainly declare our purposes and desires. Let us, like Alexander, who boldly avowed that he went for glory and conquest, declare our objects. Away with this mawkish morality." What Duer did not grasp was that "mawkish morality" was essential if the myths of Manifest Destiny were to retain their power. The American body politic could support almost any measure provided it could somehow be justified by the three great appeals—virtue, mission, destiny. It mattered little to most people that the "destiny" being asserted was, as the *American Whig Review* termed it, the "maxim that might is right—that conquest is right. . . ."

The most eloquent opponents of the war tended to be, like John Quincy Adams, aging echoes of the eighteenth-century revolutionary faith for whom Manifest Destiny was a poisonous sophistry. Preeminent among this group was Albert Gallatin, born a Swiss, adopted an American, and, with John Quincy Adams, perhaps the last voice of the Revolutionary era and the Enlightenment universalist faith. More than a half-century of public service gave Gallatin a sense of perspective sadly lacking in the young firebrands of the 1840s. The origins, conduct, and looming outcome of the war disturbed him profoundly as a renunciation of all he had worked for. In 1847, at age eighty-seven, he published the pamphlet *Peace with Mexico,* which contended that the United States was a model republic whose mission was to spread its way of life by example, not by the sword. Gallatin scathingly attacked racial justifications for the war, and even the concept of Anglo-Saxonism: "Can you for a moment suppose, that a very doubtful descent from men, who lived one thousand years ago, has transmitted to you a superiority over your fellow men?" He denied the redemptionist motives for the conquest. "The allegation that the subjugation of Mexico would be the means of enlightening the Mexicans, of improving their social state, and of increasing their happiness, is but the shallow attempt to disguise unbounded cupidity and ambition. Truth never was or can be propagated by fire and sword, or by any other then purely moral means."

The war's potential for undermining American liberty at home proved for many Americans one of the most troubling aspects of the situation. An article in the *New Englander* reiterated Gallatin's view that America's mission was to be realized by peaceful and moral means, and that the creation of invading armies foreshadowed future chaos. War caused national indebtedness, high taxes, and, most important, an increasing concentration of power, all of which undermined the very mission in whose name the war was being fought. War even frayed the presumed special relationship of the American people to God: "Just in proportion as we become a warlike people . . . we become unfit for that high function to which God manifestly calls us. . . ."

Peace with Mexico presciently observed: "Let war become the fashion of our country, and in a little while our separate States will have lost all their dignity and all the substance of their sovereignty, and the great, centralized, national government . . . will have overshadowed everything else. . . . We might have the forms of freedom still, . . . but where would be the working and the spirit of freedom?" Such consequences threatened to undermine the very nature of the Republic: "Under such a government, we should fall irretrievably from that high destiny to which the providence of God is calling us for the reformation of the world." Gallatin's poignant plea fell largely on deaf ears, the wisdom of a man whose time seemingly had passed.

In the long run, one of the most significant statements against Polk's war on Mexico was that of Henry David Thoreau of Concord, Massachusetts. Thoreau, a thirty-one-year-old teacher, surveyor, and local misfit, offered his opinions about the war and about the institution of slavery in an address delivered in February 1848 to his fellow Concordians entitled "Resistance to Civil Government." In it Thoreau probed the appropriate moral and ethical response of the individual faced with a federal authority apparently in the hands of a slaveholding, war-making clique: "Witness the present Mexican War, the work of comparatively a few individuals using the standing government as their tool; for in the outset, the people would not have consented to this measure."

Thoreau called for "honest men to rebel and revolutionize" against a state of affairs in which "a sixth of the population of a nation which has undertaken to be the refuge of liberty are slaves, and a whole country is unjustly overrun and conquered" by the United States government. Thoreau decried the "thousands of men who are in opinion opposed to slavery and to the war, who yet in effect do nothing to put an end to them," and advocated that individuals dissolve "the union between themselves and the State" by refusing to pay their quota of taxes earmarked for the federal government. Enough with petitioning, voting, and other forms of symbolic participation —they did little if anything to advance the right. In matters of extreme moral importance, as slavery and the war certainly were, the individual's responsibility was clear: ". . . Those who call themselves abolitionists should at once effectually withdraw their support, both in person and property, from the government of Massachusetts." In the name of justice and freedom, Thoreau called for secession from the Union, not by a state but by the individual. His staunch refusal to pay his own oft-requested poll tax, and the night in jail he spent for this public act of "civil disobedience," had been the incident precipitating his remarks to his fellow citizens. Now he called for all individuals of conscience to "Cast your whole vote, not a strip of paper merely, but your whole influence" by withdrawing allegiance to a state and a Union that countenanced the wickedness of a war of aggression and slavery.

Poet James Russell Lowell summarized matters this way:

They jest want this Californy
So's to lug new slave-states in
To abuse ye, an' to scorn ye
An' to plunder ye like sin. . . .

THE TREATY OF GUADELUPE HIDALGO

In the spring of 1847 Polk, evidently tired of waiting for surrender, dispatched Nicholas P. Trist as special envoy to Mexico to negotiate a treaty of peace and indemnities. The president believed that Trist, chief clerk of the State Department, would be easily managed from afar and provide a means to neutralize whatever moves General Scott might make in the name of his ambitions. Unfortunately for Polk, Trist had his own ambitions and agenda, and when he reached Scott's army it was not long before he and the general were not speaking to each other. Complicating matters further, by late 1847 Polk had decided that the nation's military successes in Mexico entitled it to far more territory than originally planned, including Baja California and the Isthmus of Tehuantepec, if not all of Mexico. Sensing that Trist might settle for only the original demands—California and New Mexico—Polk recalled his negotiator.

But Trist refused to be recalled. Having patched up his quarrel with Scott (reputedly after Scott had sent Trist a jar of guava marmalade when the diplomat was ill), Trist went to work hammering out a deal with one of the various factions contending for the role of the Mexican government. Finally, on February 2, 1848, in the village of Guadelupe Hidalgo outside Mexico City, Trist signed a treaty which, among other things, ceded California and New Mexico to the United States and confirmed once and for all the annexation of Texas, with its boundary at the Rio Grande. In exchange, the United States agreed to pay $15 million to Mexico and to assume the claims of American citizens against the Mexican government, totaling some $3 million. Trist's officially unauthorized pact arrived in Washington on February 21, 1848.

Polk, enraged by Trist's insubordination, was nonetheless in no position to withhold his treaty from Senate ratification. Whigs in the Senate had just pushed through a resolution praising the valor of General Taylor and his men in "a war unnecessarily and unconstitutionally begun by the President of the United States." Polk could not refuse to submit a treaty which, after all, did secure the original war aims. The Senate might respond to such a refusal by cutting off all war appropriations, an action it had been reluctant to take.

Hence Polk submerged his ire at being disobeyed and celebrated his treaty to the Senate, particularly its maritime advantages. He had already trumpeted the value of the West Coast in his third annual message of 1847: "The bay of San Francisco and other harbors along the Californian coast would afford shelter for our navy, for our numinous whaleships, and other merchant vessels employed in the Pacific Ocean." Polk had predicted that California ports "would in a short period become the mart of an extensive and profitable commerce with China and other countries of the East."

With the treaty in hand, he reemphasized that California and New Mexico alone "constitute of themselves a country large enough for a great empire, and their acquisition is second only in importance to that of Louisiana in 1803." California's ports, including San Diego, would "enable the United States to command an already valuable and rapidly increasing commerce of the Pacific." Indeed, access to the Pacific was the treaty's most important aspect: "In this vast region, whose rich resources are soon to be developed by American energy and enterprise, great must be the augmentation of our commerce, and with it new and valuable markets for our manufactures and agricultural products."

Thus on March 10, 1848, less than three weeks after it had arrived in Washington, a peace treaty described by one critic as "negotiated by an unauthorized agent, with an unacknowledged government, submitted by an accidental President, to a dissatisfied Senate," was ratified 38 to 14.

The war cost the United States, in addition to the $15 million payment for the territory acquired, about $100 million in war-related expenditures and more than thirteen thousand lives, fewer than two thousand of which were in battle. The war served as a training ground for an entire generation of American military heroes, including Grant, Sherman, Meade, Lee, Jackson, McClellan, and Longstreet. As these men consummated the nation's "apparent destiny" to conquer a continent, little did they know that another destiny awaited them in a conflict far grander in scale.

For Mexico the costs of the war were much greater: an estimated fifty thousand dead, loss of more than half its national territory, and widespread destruction of real estate, foodstuffs, livestock, and art treasures. Years later Ulysses S. Grant came to regret the part he had played in the conquest of Mexico: "I had the horror of the Mexican War . . . only I had not moral courage enough to resign. . . . I considered my supreme duty was to my flag."

Over the longer run the war engendered in the Mexican

people an enduring hostility to the "colossus of the north" and grievances over borders and sovereignty that persist to this day.

THE IMPERIAL CRISIS

The eloquence and prestige of much of the antiwar movement ultimately had at best a modest impact on the conduct and outcome of the war. For most Americans the principled objections and themes of self-restraint raised by the movement paled in comparison with the glorious victories in the field and the splendid domain acquired.

A far more ominous response to the expansionist gains of the war had come from Congressman David Wilmot of Pennsylvania. Wilmot, a Democrat who supported the war but was at odds with Polk, shook the foundations of the Republic in August 1846 when he introduced a rider to a military appropriations bill in the form of a resolution: "As an express and fundamental condition to the acquisition of any territory from the Republic of Mexico . . . neither slavery nor involuntary servitude shall ever exist in any part of said territory. . . ." Wilmot's motion denying the extension of slavery into the newly acquired territories struck at what many thought to be the main motive behind the acquisition of Mexican lands. After long and intense debate, near-unanimous Southern opposition in combination with a few Northern allies defeated Wilmot's Proviso. Yet for the first time a critical vote on the slavery issue had been resolved along sectional rather than party lines.

The Wilmot Proviso debate reopened the divisive question of what power, if any, the federal government had over slavery in the territories. Precedent seemed to suggest that the national government did have some jurisdiction in the matter.

The Ordinance of 1787 had banned slavery in the Old North-west, and the Missouri Compromise of 1820 had prohibited slavery in those portions of the Louisiana territory north of latitude 36 degrees, 30 minutes. Supporters represented the Wilmot Proviso as merely a new application of an established congressional prerogative. Southerners, in contrast, inter-preted the vehemence of support for the proviso as the latest sign of an ongoing effort to restrict and ultimately abolish slavery. Now, however, Senator John C. Calhoun of South Carolina began to articulate a proslavery doctrine denying the federal government any authority over slavery in the territo-ries as a denial of the property rights of the slaveholder. Cal-houn argued that only when a territory was ready for statehood could it constitutionally ban slavery.

The defeat of the Wilmot Proviso inflamed the emerging "free soil" sentiment, which feared above all else that the new regions would be inhospitable to white workingmen who were unable to afford slaves or compete economically against those who did. Unlike the abolitionists, the free-soilers cared little if at all for the plight of the slave; but they did care for their own futures and the futures of men like themselves whose economic opportunities would be seriously curtailed if slavery were extended into the new territories.

The discovery of gold in California in February 1848 meant that a divided Congress would have to confront the question of slavery in the new territories almost immediately. The gold rush precipitated a flood of fortune seekers, few of whom held slaves. California seemed likely to enter the Union as a "free" state, shifting the balance in Congress to sixteen free states, fif-teen slave. Yet the future of New Mexico and Utah remained uncertain; Southerners increasingly felt themselves and their "peculiar institution" to be under siege. No easy solution seemed in the offing. Divisiveness over the future of the imperial domain threatened to tear the nation apart. Slavery must expand or die, but to where would it expand?

In early 1850 the "great compromiser" Henry Clay, senator from Kentucky, offered to Congress a number of resolutions designed to solve the problem once and for all. As Clay fought to preserve the Union he called on God's help "to allow reason once more to assume its empire." Others were more guarded in the commitment to unity. Calhoun warned that any solution arrived at must not "reduce the question to submission or resistance" for the South; Representative Horace Mann of Massachusetts affirmed that "better disunion—better a civil or servile war—better anything that God in His Providence shall send, than an extension of slavery."

After months of agonizing debate, Clay, with the help of Senator Stephen A. Douglas of Illinois, pushed through the landmark Compromise of 1850. It bore a close resemblance to the resolutions Clay originally proposed. California was admitted as a free state, and the citizens of New Mexico and Utah were somewhat ambiguously left to decide the slavery question for themselves. The slave trade was abolished in Washington, D.C., where its existence had long been a national disgrace. Yet the compromise did not abolish slavery itself in the nation's capital.

The most controversial part of the Compromise of 1850 was a tougher Fugitive Slave Act. Northerners were now required to assist in the capture and return of runaway slaves. The law also stipulated that alleged runaways were to be tried by special commissioners instead of by jury trial. Many Northerners felt outraged at being legally obligated to assist in the hunting down of escaped slaves. Ralph Waldo Emerson described the new Fugitive Slave Act as "a filthy law" and vowed not to comply with it. Former slave and abolitionist leader Frederick Douglass, faced with being returned to bondage by the terms of the new legislation, responded more vehemently: "The only way to make the Fugitive Slave Law a dead letter is to make a half dozen or more dead kidnappers." In spite of the strong negative reaction by some, most Americans, North and South, welcomed the Compromise of 1850 as at least a temporary respite from the slavery controversy and hoped that the talk of disunion would cease. Senator Douglas proclaimed the issue permanently resolved and vowed "never to make another speech on the slavery question." Yet the expansionist ambitions of the slave power had not been satiated. Even as the dust settled around the Compromise of 1850, this clique plotted to expand into the Caribbean, with disastrous consequences for the Union.

6

Expansionists at Bay

"I want Cuba, and I know that sooner or later we must have
it. . . . I want Tamaulipas, Potosi, and one or two other
Mexican States; and I want them all for the same reason—for
the planting or spreading of slavery. . . . Yes, I want these
countries for the spread of slavery."—Senator Albert Gallatin
Brown of Mississippi, 1859

POLITICIANS AND NEWSPAPER EDITORS hailed the
Compromise of 1850 as a final resolution of the question of
slavery. Nonetheless the controversy intensified proslavery expansionist ambitions. To the defenders of slavery, the acri-
mony of the debate over the lands conquered from Mexico
and the dispute over Wilmot's Proviso made it more necessary
than ever to incorporate into the Union new lands to the
south. At stake was the balance of power within the Western
Hemisphere, the balance of power within the U.S. Senate, and
ultimately the survival of the Union.

By the early 1850s proslavery expansionists had committed
themselves to a program of Latin American imperialism. Not
that all slaveowners favored it, or that all proslavery expansionists were themselves slaveowners. The so-called slave

power had never included all slaveowners, nor would its control over national policy have been possible without the aid of Northern Democrats sympathetic to the slavery cause. Yet it was now increasingly clear to the majority of slaveowners and their sympathizers that slavery must expand or it would die, and they fought to preserve the one institution that more than any other defined Southern life. In this respect the efforts of the slave power were not so much a "conspiracy," as is sometimes suggested, as an organized effort to defend a particular interest within the Union.

To many Southerners, expansion into Latin America seemed imperative for several reasons. First, it represented a way to acquire new territories that might become slave states. In North America the Missouri Compromise line of 1820 had confined slavery to areas south of 36 degrees, 30 minutes. Within that area, the aridity of the Southwest seemed to preclude the province of New Mexico as slave territory, and California had already been admitted as a free state. To the south, Mexico blocked further expansion. Yet the acquisition of Cuba and other lands in the tropics offered boundless possibilities for new states and a chance to maintain the sectional balance in the Senate.

Proslavery advocates represented Latin American expansionism—as they had Texas earlier—as a means to "diffuse" the black population and eventually "solve" America's race problem by exporting blacks. This argument was employed to mollify whites from all sections who were wary of increasing the numbers of nonwhite citizens in the Republic.

At the same time some proslavery expansionists pushed for Latin American acquisitions as a hedge against impending disunion. If secession came, the Southern states would be strengthened by the acquisition of lands to the south, especially Cuba. Southern expansionists were not content with the status quo, especially when there was literally an army of Mexican War veterans and other assorted soldiers of fortune eager to sign on to any expedition that promised them land and status in exchange for pressing revolution in any given state.

Politically the proslavery expansionist agenda was pushed in the 1850s by Presidents Franklin Pierce and James J. Buchanan, both Northern Democrats who owed their political success to the support of the slave power. Like Polk before them, on behalf of the slave power they frankly and fervently pursued annexationist schemes in Mexico, Central America, and the Caribbean, especially Cuba. Buchanan heralded this new Manifest Destiny in his annual message to Congress in 1857: "It is beyond question the destiny of our race to spread themselves over the continent of North America. . . . The tide of emigrants will flow to the south, and nothing can eventually arrest its progress. If permitted to go there peacefully, Central America will soon contain an American population which will confer blessings and benefits as well upon the natives of their respective Governments."

Militarily the agents by which this Southern Manifest Destiny was to be realized were known as filibusters, a term applied to members of the revolution-provoking expeditions against Latin America. The word filibuster was derived from the Spanish *filibustero,* which in turn came from the Dutch *vrijbuiter*—pirate. Although some of the filibusters may have been motivated by more than mere personal gain, their actions are rightfully characterized as piratical in that they directly violated federal neutrality statutes, international law, and the sovereignty of neighbor states. Nonetheless their exploits thrilled large segments of the American press and public, which tended to invest their petty crusades with great patriotic meaning.

Filibustering expeditions were usually financed by American capitalists willing to supply ships, arms, and ammunition in exchange for promises of some form of commercial monopoly in the province to be revolutionized. A number of U.S. cities, most notably New Orleans, became bases from which military expeditions were planned, organized, and launched against targets in Mexico and the Caribbean.

Officially unauthorized private expeditions against Latin American countries were not new. As early as 1810 West Florida had been wrested from Spanish rule by a group of American emigrants who soon thereafter requested annexation to the United States. During the Latin American wars of independence, American ports had been used to outfit privateering expeditions against Spanish authority in defiance of American neutrality laws. The virtually unrestricted flow of men and materiel from the United States across the Louisiana border had made possible the success of the Texas revolution.

This tradition of exporting revolution to Latin America peaked in the 1850s when literally dozens of filibustering expeditions were launched against Mexico alone. Although they are largely forgotten today, the activities of the filibusters received extensive coverage in the press during the 1850s and were the primary foreign policy concern of presidential administrations during the period. Federal response to the filibusters varied according to circumstances and party. Whig presidents Zachary Taylor and Millard Fillmore repudiated filibusterism and sought to suppress it, without much success. Democrats Pierce and Buchanan, however, while uncomfortable with the filibusters, were inclined to reap the benefits of the filibusters' projects, particularly if this could be done without committing the prestige of the American government to an enterprise doomed to failure.

The Southern dream of Latin American empire alarmed

most Northerners. After 1848 Northern support for Southern expansionism rapidly diminished to a point where Manifest Destiny had become sectionalized. The expansionist consensus on which the Union was founded was breaking up. No longer would most Northerners acquiesce in Southern territorial gains, even if they were balanced by gains for the North.

REVOLUTIONIZING CUBA

Most of all, Southern imperialists coveted the island of Cuba. U.S. interest in the "Pearl of the Antilles" dated from colonial days when the island had been a prime source of sugar, rum, and molasses. This economic interest steadily increased in the early nineteenth century. At the same time Cuba commanded access to the Gulf of Mexico and as such was defined as an American security concern. Thomas Jefferson expressed the feelings of many when he candidly observed, "I have ever looked upon Cuba as the most interesting addition which could be made to our system of states."

Cuba's geographic proximity and economic importance to the United States prompted Secretary of State John Quincy Adams to describe the island as "an object of transcendent importance to the commercial and political interests of our Union." Adams added, "It is scarcely possible to resist the conviction that the annexation of Cuba to our federal republic will be indispensable to the continuance and integrity of the Union itself."

In instructions to the American minister in Madrid in 1823, Adams articulated what would be the nation's long-term policy when he defined Cuba as an American security issue. Foreshadowing the noncolonization principle of the Monroe Doctrine, Adams warned against Cuban sovereignty being transferred to Great Britain. More generally he asserted that "the condition of Cuba cannot be changed without affecting in an eminent degree the welfare of this Union. . . ." This tied American security to the status of Cuba. American policy presumed that in Spanish hands, one might trust in the working of time; but, as was the case with Louisiana, control over Cuba could not be changed without posing a threat to American security. In effect the United States assumed veto powers over political change in Cuba.

A variety of arguments were crafted to justify this assertion of imperialistic influence over what was a foreign land. Adams had invoked a law of "political gravitation" by which Cuba was inevitably destined to fall into the Union in the same way "an apple severed by a tempest from its native tree cannot but choose to fall to the ground." Others suggested that Cuba was little more than the accumulated siltation of the Mississippi River and as such was rightfully American territory. At times the rhetoric became more passionate. One Louisville newspaper editor claimed that Cuba "admires Uncle Sam, and he loves her. . . . Who can object if he throws his arms around the Queen of the Antilles, as she sits . . . upon the silver waves, breathing her spicy tropic breath, and pouting her rosy, sugared lips? Who can object? None. She is of age—take her, Uncle Sam!"

Cuba's importance grew as the slave question escalated. Southerners feared the "Africanization" of the island—a successful slave revolt that might spread to the United States. They also worried that Spain might abolish slavery in Cuba. However it might occur, abolition in Cuba was seen as a direct threat to slavery in North America. One Southerner predicted that "If the slave institution perishes in Cuba, it perishes here."

At the same time Cuba's fertile and abundant terrain was ideal for cotton cultivation, and only a small part of the island's soil had been tilled. Enormous profits awaited those who could efficiently exploit Cuba's resources. Moreover, Cuba might be divided into one or more new slaveholding states in order to maintain the political balance of power in Congress. More than any other territory, Cuba represented the solution to the South's greatest fears.

Thus it was with great interest that Polk received a proposal on May 10, 1848, from Senator Stephen Douglas and journalist John L. O'Sullivan that he commit his administration to the purchase of Cuba. Although the Treaty of Guadelupe Hidalgo had acquired about 500,000 square miles of new territory for the United States, Polk wanted more. He recorded his meeting with Douglas and O'Sullivan in his diary: "Though I expressed no opinion to them I am decidedly in favour of purchasing Cuba & making it one of the States of the Union." In spite of the objections of Secretary of State Buchanan and Secretary of War William L. Marcy, both of whom feared the potentially negative effect a move to acquire Cuba would have on the Democrats' fall presidential chances, Polk proceeded with his plan.

In a series of meetings with the president, O'Sullivan shared confidential knowledge of a plot by wealthy Cuban planters to rebel against Spanish authority on the island and seek annexation by the United States. Indeed, O'Sullivan's brother-in-law, Cristóbal Madan y Madan, was a leader of the Havana Club, a Masonic temple in Cuba dedicated to defending the institution of slavery on the island and seeking annexation by the United States.

Founded in the spring of 1848, the Havana Club was comprised mainly of sugar planters and aristocrats who feared the abolitionist policies being urged on Spain by England and France. These men looked to Polk and the United States as a "white knight" that might save them from the ruin of abolition. Their plan was to hire five thousand Mexican War veterans commanded by Mexican War hero and fellow Mason General William J. Worth to invade Cuba.

The conspiracy went forward in the United States largely through the efforts of Ambrosio José Gonzalez, an American-educated professor, and Narciso Lopez, a former Spanish army colonel who, for a variety of reasons, was now pledged to unremitting hostility toward Spain. Both men were members of the Havana Club. Freemasonry provided an essential link between the plotters and political and judicial circles in the United States. President Polk, Vice-President George Mifflin Dallas, Secretary of State Buchanan, and Secretary of the Navy John Y. Mason were Masons, as were Senators Douglas of Illinois and Daniel Dickinson of New York. Lopez and Gonzalez conferred with all these men in an effort to win support for their revolutionary project, and at various times they received the aid and comfort of judges, customs officials, and law enforcement personnel.

Lopez's flamboyant recklessness did not engender confidence in his prospects, either by the Havana Club or by interested Americans. In the summer of 1848 Polk, fearful that Lopez's plans might interfere with his efforts to buy the island, informed the Spanish minister to Washington of Lopez's plans to start an uprising, thereby forcing him to flee to the United States.

This allowed Polk to pursue other methods of acquiring Cuba. In instructions drafted by Buchanan to the American minister to Madrid, Romulus Saunders, on June 17, 1848, a formal rationale was articulated based on the proposition that the United States "can never consent that this island shall become a colony of any other European power." In a restatement of the No Transfer Resolution of 1811, the transfer of the island to another state was deemed potentially "ruinous" to American commerce and might "even endanger the union of the States." Cuba's strategic position, its significance in the world economy, and the question of slavery all made its acquisition essential in the view of the administration. Buchanan's instructions disingenuously claimed that fears that expansion would threaten the Union "have faded away." The American system of a confederated republic was "capable of almost indefinite extension, with increasing strength." Buchanan predicted that Cuba would soon be "Americanized" and that its acquisition "will insure the perpetuity of our Union." Saunders was empowered to offer the Spanish government as much as $100 million for the island—far more than the $15 million paid to Mexico for California and New Mexico.

The Spanish government flatly rejected Saunders's offer as an unthinkable blow to Spanish pride. "Sooner than see the island transferred," said the official reply, we would "prefer seeing it sunk in the Ocean." Thus ended Polk's plans for attaining Cuba.

Meanwhile Narciso Lopez regained his place within the Cuban revolutionary movement when General Worth was transferred to the Texas frontier and later died from cholera. The search resumed for a suitable American commander for the invasion force. Lopez approached Senator Jefferson Davis of Mississippi with a generous offer of money and land to command the invading army. Davis, also a Mexican War veteran, was determined to spread the institution of slavery to Cuba and was intrigued by the plotter's plans, but in the end he turned down the offer. He recommended instead that Lopez approach Robert E. Lee, who also rebuffed the revolutionary conspirator.

Lopez now redoubled his efforts to launch an invasion of Cuba from the United States. In an attempt to gain men and materiel, he and Gonzalez met with proslavery elements throughout the United States, including General John Quitman of Mississippi, yet another Mexican War hero. In spite of President Taylor's warning against the "armed expedition . . . about to be fitted out in the United States with the intention to invade the island of Cuba," federal officials could do little to suppress a movement that had broad public sympathy in much of the South and the active support of many well-connected individuals. In May 1850 Lopez and about five hundred mainly English-speaking mercenaries—a motley crew, motivated mostly by dreams of pillage and plunder—launched an abortive invasion of Cuba that failed to precipitate the general uprising expected. Lopez beat a quick retreat to Key West where his Masonic brothers tended his wounds and shielded him from prosecution for violation of the federal neutrality statute of 1818.

But a New Orleans grand jury did indict him for neutrality violations. This did not prevent Lopez from traveling through Georgia in search of new recruits for another planned invasion of Cuba. After being cleared of the federal charges by a friendly jury and protected from further prosecution by his network of Masonic allies in the judiciary, in the summer of 1851 Lopez launched one final effort to revolutionize Cuba. Once again his tiny invasion force found few sympathizers and soon collapsed. This time, however, Lopez did not escape. In Havana in September 1851 he was publicly garroted. Fifty captured American mercenaries were also executed by the Spanish.

The death of Lopez and the opposition of President Taylor and his successor Vice-President Millard Fillmore to Cuban annexation momentarily stilled the lust for Cuba. Fillmore made clear he regarded its addition to the Union "as fraught with serious peril." The issue was race. "Were this island destitute of inhabitants or occupied by a kindred race, I should regard it, if voluntarily ceded by Spain, as a most desirable acquisition. But under existing circumstances I should look upon its incorporation into our Union as a very hazardous measure."

Of course the Fillmore administration would not have tolerated Cuba's transfer to any other European state, but short of that it preferred to await the operation of time to resolve the Cuban question. Fillmore's secretary of state, Edward Everett, warned the French government to keep hands off: "The President does not covet the acquisition of Cuba for the United States; at the same time, he considers the condition of Cuba as mainly an American question."

The ascension of Franklin Pierce to the presidency in 1853 saw the renewal of the campaign to acquire Cuba. Pierce was a "doughface," a slang term used to describe a Northerner with Southern sympathies. His inaugural address made clear his priorities: he pledged that his administration would "not be controlled by any timid forebodings of evil from expansion" and declared that "our attitude as a nation and our position on the globe render the acquisition of certain possessions . . . important for our protection, if not in the future essential for the preservation of the rights of commerce and the peace of the world."

Pierce's election encouraged Southerners to rekindle their efforts to launch an invasion of Cuba that would expel the Spanish and prepare the way for annexation along the lines of the Texas model. New Orleans buzzed with the rumors of a filibustering army of as many as fifty thousand men, led by John Quitman, that planned to invade Cuba. Quitman and his supporters evidently proceeded with their plans with at least the tacit support of the Pierce administration, which showed no tendency to prevent the expedition from departing. The situation escalated in late 1853 when rumors flew that the Spanish planned to abolish slavery in Cuba—a prelude to the dreaded "Africanization" of the island that would occur when the white population fled. The governor of Louisiana warned of the impending creation of a government "administered by an inferior and barbarous race under the immediate influence of European interests and ideas."

Political tensions created by the debate over the Kansas-Nebraska Act in early 1854 prompted Pierce to withdraw his support of the Quitman expedition. The president now decided to renew the offer to purchase Cuba and to take it by force if Spain again refused to sell. In April Secretary of State William L. Marcy instructed Minister to Spain Pierre Soulé of Louisiana to approach the Spanish with a new offer. Soulé was given "full power" to purchase Cuba and authorized to spend as much as $130 million to do so—a figure substantially higher than the 1848 offer of $100 million. Marcy anticipated that although "pride" might prevent Spain from selling the island, perhaps the Spanish could be enticed to grant Cuba its independence before annexation by the United States. Soulé had announced upon his departure to Spain, "I hope when I return to see a new star shine in the celestial vault of young America."

Soulé's brashness destroyed what little possibility existed that Spain would sell Cuba. In the wake of his rebuff, Soulé traveled to Ostend, Belgium, in October 1854 to confer with the American ministers to England and France, James Buchanan and John Y. Mason. There the trio schemed to make Cuban annexation a reality. Their recommendations were made known in a secret communication to the president that became known as the Ostend Manifesto. The result, leaked to the public soon after its drafting, was a diplomatic bombshell. It was premised on the conviction that "an immediate and earnest effort ought to be made" by the United States to purchase Cuba from Spain "at any price for which it

can be obtained." At any price! The American ministers unc-
tuously expressed confidence that Spain would sell "because
this would essentially promote the highest and best interests of
the Spanish people."

More to the point, the ministers asserted that Cuba was as
"necessary to the North American republic as any of its present members, and that it belongs naturally to that great family
of States of which the Union is the providential nursery." As
was the case in so many prior declarations regarding Cuba,
the integrity of the United States was linked to the island:
" . . . the Union can never enjoy repose, nor possess reliable security, as long as Cuba is not embraced within its boundaries."
The ministers warned that it would be "exceedingly dangerous" for the United States to delay its acquisition owing to unsettled conditions on the island.

But the three diplomats saved for the conclusion their most
audacious recommendation. Should Spain for some reason
refuse peacefully to transfer Cuba, then "by every law human
and divine, we shall be justified in wresting it from Spain"—
upon the same principle, they claimed, that would justify a
person in "tearing down the burning house of his neighbor if
there were no other means of preventing the flames from de-
stroying his own home." As outrageous as it sounded, this was
the same rationale by which Florida had been obtained a
quarter-century earlier, and under different circumstances
might have proved equally persuasive.

By 1854, however, the rationales of Manifest Destiny provoked more controversy than consensus in the public mind.
In the minds of many Americans, expansion was now inextri-
cably tied to slavery. Newspaper editor Horace Greeley described the report of Soulé, Buchanan, and Mason as the
"manifesto of the brigands." Opposition to Cuban annexation
had been growing in parallel to the intensifying debate over

slavery. Representative Gerrit Smith of New York proclaimed to the Senate that "Never has there been so self-deceived a nation as our own. That we are a nation for liberty is among our wildest conceits." Representative Milton S. Latham of California had expressed concern about those individuals "to whose peculiar keeping it would seem an overruling Providence had confided the destinies of a great Republic!" Latham anticipated Spain's departure from Cuba but called for annexation in a "quiet, orderly, direct way, without noise or bluster."

For other Americans, the idea of Manifest Destiny retained its power to inspire. An 1850 article in *DeBow's Review* justified Lopez's efforts by appeals to the past: "The history of the world furnishes no instance of a great and growing power intent on pursuing its career of progress and improvement without encroaching upon the right and dominions of weaker neighbors." Another article in the same journal took a different view of matters: "Much nonsense has been said of our manifest destiny. . . . The thief thinks it is his destiny when he picks your pocket or steals your horse. . . . Our true destiny . . . is to do justice to others, and to see that justice is done to us."

The controversy over the Ostend Manifesto effectively ended the possibility of acquiring Cuba. Although James Buchanan listed its annexation as one of the goals of his administration in his inaugural address in 1857, little came of his efforts owing to the impasse over slavery. As late as 1859 the Senate Foreign Relations Committee chaired by John Slidell of Louisiana issued a report stating that "the ultimate acquisition of Cuba may be considered a fixed purpose" of the United States. The report boldly declared, "The law of our national existence is growth. We cannot, if we would, disobey it." Yet the breakdown of the expansionist consensus meant that consummation of the long-held desire to control Cuba would have to wait until the close of the nineteenth century.

CONTENDING FOR A CANAL

From the moment the United States annexed California in 1848, control of an isthmian crossing through Central America became of the utmost importance. In the days before the transcontinental railroad, access to the West Coast was faster, easier, and cheaper via Central America than it was by wagon train across the vast expanses of North America. The discovery of gold in California and the subsequent "rush" to the gold fields magnified the importance of an isthmian crossing. Attention was focused on three possible routes: Panama, which remained a part of Colombia, then known as New Granada; Nicaragua, where most of the journey across the isthmus could already be made by boat; and Tehuantepec in southern Mexico, where dangerous offshore currents made it less attractive than the other two sites.

Polk recognized the critical importance of an isthmian canal and acted to assert a U.S. presence in Central America. Treasury Secretary Robert J. Walker summarized the geoeconomic possibilities: "Our maritime frontier upon the Pacific is now nearly equal to our Atlantic Coast, with many excellent bays and harbors, admirably situated to command the trade of Asia and the whole western coast of America." Linking the East and West coasts via an isthmian crossing would facilitate "in time, the command of the trade of the world."

Polk's first move in the region had been through the efforts of American diplomat Benjamin Bidlack, who in 1846 negotiated a treaty with Colombia for access rights across the Isthmus of Panama. The Bidlack Treaty gave the United States the right of way along the crossing, but Colombia retained sovereignty over the region.

While Panama offered the shortest route between the two oceans, its rugged terrain presented a formidable barrier to a canal. More promising was a crossing in Nicaragua, where Lake Nicaragua and the San Juan River already offered a water route across most of the way. Once again, however, American expansionism collided with the lion of British imperialism. British interests in the region dated from the sixteenth century when they had colonized a portion of the Honduran coast for its timber supply. By 1848 they had established a "protectorate" over the Miskito Indians on Nicaragua's Atlantic coast and had seized the village of Greytown at the mouth of the San Juan River, thereby gaining control of any potential isthmian crossing. At the western end of the prospective crossing, British agents acted to block U.S. access by occupying the strategically important Tigre Island, thereby preventing American firms from beginning work on a canal.

Meanwhile Elijah Hise had been dispatched by Washington to Nicaragua, where he successfully negotiated a treaty giving the United States exclusive control over a canal site and concessions for American firms involved in its construction. A second American emissary, Ephraim G. Squier, negotiated with Honduras a treaty ceding to the United States control of Tigre Island—the same spot occupied by the British. By 1850 the United States and Great Britain appeared heading toward a confrontation over control of an isthmian crossing.

Confrontation was avoided when Secretary of State John Clayton and British Minister to the United States Sir Henry Lytton Bulwer negotiated an end to the controversy. The Clayton-Bulwer Treaty of 1850 pledged both nations not to "ever obtain or maintain for itself any exclusive control" over any canal, nor would either "occupy, fortify, or colonize, or assume or exercise any dominion" over any part of Central America. The pact is noteworthy as one of the few examples in American history of the United States agreeing not to seek control over a region in the Western Hemisphere. From the time that John Quincy Adams rebuffed Lord Canning's 1823 proposal of a joint declaration eschewing further expansion in the Western Hemisphere, it had been a basic principle of American diplomacy to refrain from such arrangements. Indeed, construction of the Panama Canal required that the Clayton-Bulwer Treaty be repealed. But in 1850 it tempered a potentially volatile situation and defused the threat of war.

Still, the treaty did not solve all points of controversy. American firms still pushed for a greater say in the development of an isthmian crossing, and the British still maintained their "protectorate" over the Miskito Indians, which they claimed was valid under the Clayton-Bulwer Treaty as a preexisting possession. In early 1853 the Greytown town council, with British backing, evicted Cornelius Vanderbilt's Accessory Transit Company from its office in Punta Arenas. Vanderbilt, a millionaire shipping magnate from New York, appealed to Washington for help. By mid-February the sloop of war USS *Cyane,* commanded by Captain George N. Hollins, had arrived on the scene to defend Vanderbilt's property rights. Hollins informed local authorities that further efforts to dislodge or harass the company would be met with force.

The bad feelings engendered by this incident were considerably worsened by the arrival of Solon Borland as U.S. minister to Nicaragua. Borland, a former senator from Arkansas and an ardent slavery expansionist, made no secret of his wish to see the Clayton-Bulwer Treaty repealed and Nicaragua annexed to the United States.

An incident soon occurred that sparked a major confrontation. After the American transit steamer *Routh* accidentally struck a Nicaraguan fishing boat, the boat's black master energetically demanded indemnity for damages. The sauciness of the request prompted homicidal rage in the *Routh*'s commander, who allegedly declared, "I must shoot this fellow. He has used threatening language that shall cost him his life"—and shot the man dead. Efforts by the Nicaraguans to arrest both the commander and Minister Borland for the murder sent Borland fleeing to Washington for protection and representatives of the Accessory Transit Company pleading for reparations for property losses.

The *Cyane,* which had temporarily departed, was soon on its way back to Nicaragua. Captain Hollins's instructions informed him that "it is very desirable that these people should be taught that the United States will not tolerate these outrages, and that they have the power and the determination to check them." Hollins demanded that the town council of Greytown pay indemnities to the American firm and issue an apology. When he received no response, Hollins opened fire on Greytown. In three separate bombardments on July 13, 1853, the *Cyane*'s guns destroyed Greytown. Accessory Transit Company officials greedily anticipated the aftermath. An attorney for the company wrote to one of its agents, "If the scoundrels are soundly punished, we can take possession, and build it up as a business place, put in our own officers, transfer the jurisdiction, and you know the rest."

The brutality of the assault on Greytown provoked widespread condemnation in the United States and elsewhere. British Lord Clarenden described it as an outrage "without parallel in the annals of modern times." The *New York Tribune* deemed the attack as "a needless, unjustifiable, unhuman exercise of warlike force." Even Secretary of State Marcy was shocked by the violence. He wrote to Minister Buchanan in London, "The place merited chastisement, but the severity of the one inflicted exceeded all expectations."

Yet President Pierce, sensing the larger issues of imperial control at stake, supported Hollins's actions. Pierce, as was so often the case in such affairs, placed full responsibility for the destruction on the residents of Greytown, which he characterized as a "pretended community . . . composed for the most part of blacks and persons of mixed blood" given to "mischievous and dangerous propensities." Pierce stood by the assault, confident that the British public and its government would not choose to disrupt relations with their largest trading partner over the deaths of native peoples in a distant colony. Pierce's assumption proved correct, and the event passed unlamented into America's past.

WALKER IN NICARAGUA

There now appeared on the stage the most famous filibuster of all—William Walker of Tennessee. Walker was a failed doctor, lawyer, and newspaperman who had come to California as a young man seeking success. In 1853 he led an abortive invasion of Sonora, Mexico, that resulted in his being tried in San Francisco for violation of federal neutrality statutes. Acquitted of those charges by a friendly jury, Walker was soon approached by Byron Cole, a San Francisco capitalist with mining investments in Nicaragua that were threatened by civil strife. Cole hired Walker to lead a column of fifty-eight men—styled by Walker as "the immortals"—to intervene in the Nicaraguan civil war and help safeguard Cole's investments.

But Walker saw himself as far more than just a caretaker of someone else's investments. Once in Nicaragua he moved to seize control of the government and establish himself as the law of the land. Slightly built and authoritarian in command—one follower described him a "freckled-faced despot"—Walker nonetheless exuded a charisma that inspired loyalty. At the same time he was not reluctant to execute those he deemed to be lacking in loyalty. By October 1855 he had cleverly exploited divisions within the various factions and made himself dictator of Nicaragua. He then petitioned Washington for recognition.

Walker promoted his cause through the creation of *El Nicaraguense,* a newspaper whose main purpose was to dispatch heroic tales of Walker's revolutionary exploits to the United States. *El Nicaraguense* called Walker "the grey-eyed man of destiny" that local legends foretold would redeem Nicaragua's Indians from despotism. In fact Walker envisioned the creation of a new despotism, a Central American slave empire, headed by himself. Its eventual annexation by the United States would confirm Walker's ambition of being one of the great nation-builders in American history.

Although the Pierce administration hesitated to recognize Walker's regime, his exploits soon made him a national favorite—"the greatest hero of his age," as one newspaper described him. Walker's September 1856 proclamation reinstituting slavery in Nicaragua confirmed his stature in the South. The move was calculated, he said, to bind "the Southern states to Nicaragua as if she were one of themselves." At the same time Walker played to North American fears and loathings by casting himself in the role of challenger to British imperialism in Central America. His widely publicized exploits spurred a plank in the 1856 Democratic party platform sympathizing with "the efforts being made by the people of Central America to regenerate that portion of the continent which covers the passage across the interoceanic isthmus."

Even as the Pierce administration responded to Walker's growing acclaim by moving to recognize his regime, Walker was forced from power by a coalition of forces from the other Central American republics and by the hostility of Vanderbilt, whose interests in the region Walker had challenged. In mid-1857 Walker fled Nicaragua and returned to the United States where he was lavishly feted as one of slavery's greatest champions. He played to the crowd, telling a Mobile audience that he sought to "extend your institutions," meaning slavery. He predicted to fellow slavery expansionists that "the pure Indian race" of Nicaragua could "be made slaves, in cases of Americans becoming conquerors and masters there." Walker's book *The War in Nicaragua* called for the establishment of a "slave empire" in Central America as the only means "short of revolution" by which the South might protect slavery.

Walker mounted a second expedition against Nicaragua, which failed in November 1857 when Commodore Hiram Paulding deployed U.S. marines to block Walker's intended voyage up the San Juan River of Nicaragua. In spite of the doubtful legality of enforcing American law on foreign soil, Paulding arrested Walker and returned him to the United States to face prosecution for violating federal neutrality statutes.

Paulding's actions outraged the Southern press, which demanded that the Buchanan administration free Walker, compensate him for his losses, and punish Commodore Paulding for exceeding his authority. A Knoxville paper accused Buchanan of desiring to "crush out the expansion of slavery to the South. They know that the movement of Walker is intimately connected with the slave interests of the entire South." For both jurisdictional and political reasons, the charges against Walker were soon dropped.

Although he was not prosecuted, Walker's arrest by an agent of the U.S. government was seen as a direct challenge to slavery expansionism and precipitated an intense debate in Congress, where certain members characterized Walker as a tool of the slave power. In response to these charges, Representative William T. Avery of Tennessee declared that "in my judgment, a heavier blow was never struck at southern rights, southern interests, the advancement, the fulfillment of our great American destiny, than when Commodore Paulding perpetrated upon our people his high-handed outrage." Walker, a troubled individual of uncertain motives, had become a potent symbol of the impending struggle over slavery.

Kept in the public eye by the congressional hearings, Walker had no trouble raising funds for a third expedition against Nicaragua in December 1858. This too failed miserably when his flagship ran aground sixty miles off the Central American coast. His prestige now waning, in 1860 Walker attempted once more to revolutionize Nicaragua, this time by landing in Honduras and marching overland. In September he was captured by a British naval officer and turned over to the Hondurans, who condemned "the grey-eyed man of destiny" to face a firing squad. So ended the career of the most notorious filibuster of all.

Although Walker failed in his efforts to create a Central American slave empire, his actions intensified the domestic debate over slavery. Prominent Southern political leaders, especially those from the Gulf states, embraced him as an icon. Northerners vilified him for the same reason. Southern dissatisfaction with the Union increased because of the explicit Northern resistance to Walker's endeavors, leading Senator Albert Gallatin Brown of Mississippi to suggest that the North's refusal to allow slavery to expand southward was it-

self sufficient cause for secession. Walker became a martyr to
the cause of the South's Caribbean imperialism.

EXPANSIONISTS AT BAY

No new territories were added to America's imperial domain between the end of the Mexican War and the beginning
of the Civil War, with the exception of a 29,000-square-mile
section along the Gila River in Arizona, purchased in 1853
from Mexico. The so-called Gadsden Purchase was designed
to feed Southern ambitions by providing a railroad route to
the Pacific. Yet in spite of the agitation of slave power and the
expeditions of the filibusters, the South's campaign to expand
into Latin America failed, stymied by a rising opposition to
the further extension of slavery.

From the time of the Constitutional Convention, the place
of slavery in the nation and the empire had been controversial.
It was the one fundamental difference of interest in the Union
that did not respond to appeals to the common good. The expansionist consensus that had formed the basis of the Union
had survived several imperial crises by a careful balancing of
interests. Differences over how to divide the Louisiana territory threatened to destroy the Union until the Missouri Compromise seemed to offer a formula permanently to resolve the
question. In 1819 the issue of slavery had induced Monroe and
Adams to concede the American claim to Texas rather than
introduce its destabilizing influence into national politics in
the wake of the Missouri crisis. After the independence of
Texas, annexation had been delayed for nine years owing to
the fears of Jackson and others of its divisive effects. Texas finally was admitted to the Union by the constitutionally dubious means of joint resolution, and then only when balanced by
Oregon.

The Compromise of 1850 had resolved the debate over what to do with the lands conquered from Mexico. But that was the last accommodation. The moral pleas of the abolitionists were now joined by the self-interested concerns of a rising antislavery majority in the Northern states that by 1856 coalesced into the new Republican party. The Republicans were founded on the principle that slavery was an economic threat to the average white man and as such must be prevented from spreading. One newspaperman put the matter this way: "I am opposed to slavery not because it is a misery to the downtrodden and oppressed slave, but because it blights and mildews the white man whose lot is toil, and whose capital is his labor."

To the opponents of slavery extension, the issue also went far beyond domestic politics, posing a threat to the fulfillment of America's world-redeeming destiny. Abraham Lincoln affirmed this in 1854 when he wrote that "slavery deprives our republican example of its just influence in the world—enables the enemies of free institutions to taunt us as hypocrites." Republican Senator Charles Sumner of Massachusetts agreed that slavery "degrades our country, and prevents its example from being all-conquering." Slavery must be ended so that the United States could continue on in its mission of the "universal restoration of power to the governed." Republican radical Salmon P. Chase defined the issue of slavery in the imperial domain as a series of choices: "freedom not serfdom; freeholds not tenancies; democracy not despotism; education not ignorance."

Thus two different types of freedom contended, one based on slave labor and one based on free labor. These notions of freedom clashed in the imperial domain, where Republican Senator William Seward of New York predicted the nation would "finally decide whether this is to be the land of slavery or of freedom." To Seward and other Republican leaders, slavery was a fatal obstacle to the realization of the Union's transcendent mission to regenerate the world, a barrier to America assuming its rightful place among the world's major powers.

Hence the Republicans were determined at any cost to stop the acquisition of more potential slave territory as the most effective way to achieve abolition. Newspaperman Horace Greeley noted this in 1856: "To restrict slavery within its present limits is to secure its speedy decline and ultimate extinction." Senator Carl Schurz of Missouri observed in 1858 that in the opinions of slaveholders themselves, "slavery cannot thrive, unless it be allowed to expand. . . . Well, then, . . . pent it up!" In 1860 Senator Oliver P. Morton put matters even more concisely: "If we do not exclude slavery from the Territories, it will exclude us."

Slavery expansionists understood this point with equal clarity. Slavery did need to expand in order to survive. The failure to annex Cuba, Nicaragua, or other lands to the south made it abundantly clear that although the slave power controlled the national government, antislavery forces would veto the acquisition of potential slave states in an attempt to confine it. Daniel Barringer of North Carolina acknowledged this when he observed that "when slavery is gathered into a cul-de-sac, and surrounded by a wall of free states, it is destroyed. Slavery must have expansion. It must expand by the acquisition of territory which we now do not own."

DESTINY DISCLOSED

By 1860 the United States had expanded across a continent, achieved strategic supremacy in the Western Hemisphere, and established the foundations of a twentieth-century global empire. The dreams of the nation's founders had been realized and in many respects surpassed. A divine destiny did seem to have been achieved, and at comparatively little cost in blood or treasure.

Yet a counterdestiny now awaited fulfillment. Almost from the start, predictions of disunion and civil war had been common in American politics. Every crisis had prompted murmurings of secession which increased in number and in intensity with the passage of time. Repeated attempts to muffle, repress, or literally "gag" debate over the one issue that more than any other threatened to destroy the Union had failed. In 1858 Seward described matters in stark terms: "It is an irrepressible conflict between opposing and enduring forces, and it means that the United States must and will, sooner or later, become either entirely a slave-holding nation, or entirely a free-labor nation. . . ."

Given this stark choice, it is understandable that the election of the Republican Abraham Lincoln to the presidency in 1860 precipitated the withdrawal of the Deep South from the Union. Proslavery forces had controlled the national government almost without interruption from the time of Jackson. Now the government was controlled by a man and a party unambiguously opposed to the extension of slavery, and who had received less than 1 percent of the vote in the Southern states. Lincoln's inflexibility on the issue of nonextension left little room for compromise and signaled a death warrant for the "peculiar institution."

Thus it was not surprising when Lincoln rejected Kentucky Senator John Crittenden's compromise plan to save the Union by permanently guaranteeing slavery south of the Missouri Compromise line in all lands currently held and "hereafter acquired." On January 11, 1861, the president-elect observed that ". . . if we surrender [to Crittenden's proposal], it is the end of us, and of the government. They [the South] will repeat the experiment upon us *ad libitum*. A year will not pass, til we shall have to take Cuba, as a condition upon which we stay in the Union." Republican Senator Roscoe Conkling of New York attacked the "hereafter clause" as "a perpetual covenant of war against every people, tribe, and state . . . between here and Tierra del Fuego. It would make the government the armed missionary of slavery. . . ."

Although the Union of states had been formed on the basis of the consent of its members, time and events had transformed it into much more than the mere sum of its parts. From a loose confederacy of states it had evolved into one nation with a world-redeeming mission from which there could be no withdrawal. With Manifest Destiny realized at relatively little cost, a second destiny now awaited, less apparent but no less real than the first, to confirm the permanence of the American nation and empire at the cost of 600,000 lives.

Suggested Reading

ON THE pre-Revolutionary, Revolutionary, and Federalist eras, see Richard W. Van Alstyne, *Empire and Independence: The International History of the American Revolution* (New York, 1965); Gerald Stourzh, *Benjamin Franklin and American Foreign Policy*, 2nd ed. (Chicago, 1969); and Gordon S. Wood, *The Radicalism of the American Revolution* (New York, 1992).

On the Jeffersonian era, see George A. Dangerfield, *The Era of Good Feelings* (New York, 1952); William Appleman Williams, *The Contours of American History* (Cleveland, 1961); Roger H. Brown, *The Republic in Peril: 1812* (New York, 1964); Drew McCoy, *The Elusive Republic: Political Economy in Jeffersonian America* (Chapel Hill, 1980); Steven Watts, *The Republic Reborn: War and the Making of Liberal America, 1790–1820* (Baltimore, 1987); Robert W. Tucker and David C. Hendrickson, *Empire of Liberty: The Statecraft of Thomas Jefferson* (New York, 1990); and William Earl Weeks, *John Quincy Adams and American Global Empire* (Lexington, Ky., 1992).

For a comprehensive overview of the period between the War of 1812 and the Civil War, see Richard W. Van Alstyne, *The Rising American Empire* (New York, 1960), and Paul A. Varg, *United States Foreign Relations, 1820–1860* (East Lansing, Mich., 1979). On American commercial expansionism, see Vernon G. Setser, *The Commercial Reciprocity Policy of the United States, 1774–1829* (Philadelphia, 1937); James A. Field, Jr., *America and the Mediterranean World, 1776–1882* (Princeton, 1969); William H. Becker and Samuel F. Wells, Jr., *Economics and World Power: An Assessment of American Diplomacy Since 1789* (New York, 1984); John M. Belohlavek, *"Let the Eagle Soar!": The Foreign Policy of Andrew Jackson* (Lincoln, Nebr., 1985); Norman E. Saul, *Distant*

Friends: The United States and Russia, 1763–1867 (Lawrence, Kans., 1991); and Arthur Power Dudden, *The American Pacific: From the Old China Trade to the Present* (New York, 1992).

On the idea of Manifest Destiny, see Albert K. Weinberg, *Manifest Destiny: A Study of Nationalist Expansionism* (Baltimore, 1935); Reginald Horsman, *Race and Manifest Destiny. The Origins of American Racial Anglo-Saxonism* (Cambridge, Mass., 1981). On the role of women in American foreign policy, see Edward M. Crapol, *Women and American Foreign Policy: Lobbyists, Critics, and Insiders,* 2nd ed. (Wilmington, Del., 1992). On the role of the navy, see John H. Schroeder, *Shaping a Maritime Empire: The Commercial and Diplomatic Role of the American Navy, 1829–1861* (Westport, Conn., 1985).

On the 1840s, see Frederick Merk, *Manifest Destiny and Mission in American History* (New York, 1963), and Thomas R. Hietala, *Manifest Design: Anxious Aggrandizement in Late Jacksonian America* (Ithaca, 1985). On the Mexican War, see Robert E. May, *John A. Quitman: Old South Crusader* (Baton Rouge, 1985).

On westward expansion, see Earl Pomeroy, *The Pacific Slope: A History of California, Oregon, Washington, Idaho, Utah and Nevada* (New York, 1965); Norman A. Graebner, *Empire on the Pacific: A Study in American Continental Expansion,* reprint ed. (Santa Barbara, Calif., 1983); and William H. Goetzmann, *New Lands, New Men: America and the Second Great Age of Discovery* (New York, 1986).

On the filibuster movement, see Charles H. Brown, *Agents of Manifest Destiny: The Lives and Times of the Filibusters* (Chapel Hill, 1980). On Southern imperialism, see Robert E. May, *The Southern Dream of a Caribbean Empire, 1854–1861* (Baton Rouge, 1973).

Index

A NOTE ON THE AUTHOR

William Earl Weeks was born and grew up in Baltimore, and later studied at the University of California, San Diego, where he received a Ph.D. in American history. He now teaches American history at San Diego State University. His writings on early American diplomatic history include *John Quincy Adams and American Global Empire.*